Get a Kick Out of Life

Get a Kick Out of Life

WITHOUT BRUISING YOURSELF

by

Wendy B. Gardner

XULON PRESS

Xulon Press
2301 Lucien Way #415
Maitland, FL 32751
407.339.4217
www.xulonpress.com

Unless otherwise indicated, Scripture quotations taken from the King
James Version (KJV) – *public domain*.

Printed in the United States of America.

ISBN-13: 978-1-6305-0443-4

To my father, Edward Barrus, who viewed the world through rose colored glasses and shared the lenses with me.

TABLE OF CONTENTS

INTRODUCTION

"Life is to be enjoyed, not just endured."
President Gordon B. Hinckley

Notice the title of this book is, *Get a Kick Out of Life **Without Bruising Yourself**.* It is *not* titled, *Get a Kick Out of Life Without **Getting Bruised**.* We all recognize the impossibility of experiencing this life without bruises. Life comes with some lumps, disappointments, illnesses and sorrows. "It must needs be, that there is an opposition in all things" (2 Nephi 2:11).

We could compare life to Cream of Wheat Cereal. It might be a bit of a stretch, but walk with me to the stove for a moment. Those who are new to the experience of making Cream of Wheat usually expect to find a nice smooth cereal that looks like the picture on the box. They follow the directions, carefully pour the cereal in the boiling water and slowly stir. But just as they are ready to transfer the cereal to a bowl, they notice a lump.

That is how life is, too. Most of us move along the pathway of life following the directions and hoping for smooth and even trails. What we find, however, is that in spite of our efforts, we encounter a few bumps that cause us to fall and become bruised. Our *reaction* to those lumps and bumps is the important part.

Let's go back to the cereal for a minute. Let's say that breakfast eater #1 was so frustrated at the lumps in her cereal that she threw the contents of her bowl into the garbage disposal refusing to eat any breakfast at all. Breakfast eater #2 watched what happened to #1 and refused to try making the cereal for fear that he would make a mistake and cause a lump to form. Breakfast eater # 3 hid the lumps in her cereal from the other eaters and told them her cereal had turned out perfectly. Breakfast eater #4 tried making the cereal again, but didn't make any adjustments. Consequently, he got the same results. Furthermore, he whined to breakfast eater's #1-3 hoping for their sympathy. Breakfast eater #5 ignored the lumps and swallowed everything with a smile on her face. She then quietly slunk into another room where she drank an entire bottle of Pepto Bismol. Breakfast eater #6 enjoyed the smooth part of the cereal, then asked for help from some more experienced cooks on how to manage the lumpy part.

Granted, the cereal analogy sounds a little mushy. But if we are willing to take a closer look and examine how we approach situations or relationships in our lives, we may come to realize some similarities. The lumps are what life sometimes brings to the boiling pot. They represent those circumstances over which we have no control. The breakfast eaters represent our approach to life. Obviously, some strategies are better than others in allowing us to enjoy the smooth goodness in between the lumps. President Russell M. Nelson provides an excellent one: "When the focus of our lives is on Jesus Christ and His gospel, we can feel joy regardless of what is happening–or not happening–in our lives" ("Joy and Spiritual Survival," LDS General Conference, Oct. 2016).

Sometimes, in order to better focus on Jesus Christ, we have to eliminate a few obstacles that mar our vision. Those obstacles can be our own negative habits. At the same time, however, we need to be "filling our lamps with oil" so as to prepare ourselves for the storms that may rage against us.

By recognizing how we approach our efforts to Come Unto Christ, we can strengthen our resolve and success in doing just that. Perhaps the messages in these chapters will provide inspiration that will help in enjoying the smooth goodness and joy of life—in spite of the lumps we may encounter.

Am I Perfect Yet?

"Be ye therefore perfect, even as your Father which is in heaven is perfect" (Matthew 5:48). That scripture sounds daunting, doesn't it? But, isn't every individual, family or business striving to reach a perfect goal? Don't we want our children to be the best at whatever they attempt? Doesn't a growing business offer its employees incentives based on their record-breaking accomplishments? Don't we make goals in our journal for this year and next year and the next? Don't we practice over and over again until we perform to perfection? No one wakes up in the morning and says, "Okay, I think I'll do a mediocre job on that report today," or "I think I'll yell at the kids at least twelve times before lunch." No one makes plans based on failure. We plan to succeed. As Christians, our ultimate success equals personal perfection. We desire to enter into the Celestial Kingdom and be in the presence of Heavenly Father and Jesus Christ. So perhaps it is not perfection that needs to be examined so much as our *perception* of perfection.

Attaining Perfection

President Joseph Fielding Smith gives a helpful explanation of the process involved when working toward perfection: "I believe the Lord meant just what he said: that we should be perfect, as our Father in Heaven is perfect. That will not come all at once, but line upon line, and precept upon precept, example upon example, and even then not as long as we live in this mortal life, for we will have to go even beyond the grave before we reach that perfection and shall be like God" (*Doctrines of Salvation*, comp. Bruce R. McConkie, 3 vols. Salt Lake City: Bookcraft, 1954-56, 2:18-19).

Elder Marvin J. Ashton continues to clarify: "We need to come to terms with our desire to reach perfection and our frustration when our accomplishments or behaviors are less than perfect. I feel that one of the great myths we would do well to dispel is that we've come to earth to perfect ourselves, and nothing short of that will do. If I understand the teachings of the prophets of this dispensation correctly, we will not become perfect in this life, though we can make significant strides toward that goal" ("On Being Worthy," *Ensign*, May 1989, 20).

Elder Bruce R. McConkie gives this understanding: "We have to become perfect to be saved in the celestial kingdom. But nobody becomes perfect in this life. Only the Lord Jesus attained that state and he had an advantage that none of us has. He was the Son of God... Becoming perfect in Christ is a process" (*1976 Devotional Speeches of the Year*, Provo: Brigham Young University Press, 1977, 399-400).

These statements help clarify that it is our duty to *work toward* perfection. But as we move along that path, we will surely stumble. We can give up and take another path, we can blame God or our family or the Church for our pains, or we can recognize the pitfalls and make the necessary adjustments. We then continue to move toward our goal of perfection. Although we may not reach that in all things, we can be perfect in our obedience of certain commandments and then challenge ourselves to work for the perfection of others.

The key verbs in that paragraph are *recognize, adjust* and *work*. Those actions are to be used over and over again as we move forward. Everyone in the Church is asked and expected to do just that, from the apostle to the deacon and the Relief Society President to the Primary child.

Working toward perfection requires effort, but just as often it requires us to recognize when we need to alter our direction. Admitting that we are not perfect, allows us an opportunity to repent and make the needed adjustments that will enable us to come closer to perfection.

Elder Jeffery R. Holland reminds us, "Our only hope for true perfection is in receiving it as a gift from heaven–we can't "earn" it....If we persevere, then somewhere in eternity our refinement will be finished and complete–which is the New Testament meaning of *perfection*" ("Be Ye Therefore Perfect–Eventually," LDS General Conference, Oct. 2017).

Perfection vs. Perfectionism

In contrast, examine this definition of *perfectionism* from Elder Cecil O. Samuelson: "Perfectionism is a medical condition characterized by severe self-criticism and self-doubt, often accompanied by anxiety, depression, or obsessive-compulsive behavior. It can lead to appetite and sleep disturbances, confusion, problems in relationships, inability to concentrate, procrastination of important tasks, and, if left untreated, major depression, anxiety disorders, and suicide" ("What Does It Mean to Be Perfect?" *New Era*, Jan. 2006, 12). If we are talking about the pursuit of excellence, this is the unhealthy way to approach it. It does not allow for mistakes; it is the irrational belief that either you or your environment must always be perfect.

Some may view working toward perfection as a son or daughter in the Lord's Kingdom as a separate experience from our daily personal and social activities. It is all interrelated. We have perceptions of how "perfect" people should look and act, how they should conduct their lives, and which activities should take up their children's time. If we are to believe the mainstream American media, all women should be a size six and all men must look like a movie star. All children should get 4.0 grade point averages, all sons will be the star quarterback, all daughters will be the homecoming queen, all marriages will be like Cinderella's, all fathers will be doctors or lawyers and all mothers will be a combination of Betty Crocker, Miss America and Judge Judy. We must all smile with our perfectly straight, white teeth and walk with our toned abs and appear that all is well with the world. That perception of perfection is unhealthy and damaging to the individuals and societies who promote it. If we work harder at projecting an outward image of ourselves than we do of working toward a better self, we will surely become exhausted.

I recognized some of these tendencies in myself when I was serving as Young Women President in our ward. My attempt to magnify my calling was sometimes overshadowed by my attempt to appear spectacular. I wanted to do my best, of course. I made color-coded three-month calendars for each young woman and presented one to the bishop at youth council. I had color-coded tablecloths for each value, along with a matching centerpiece. I always wrote the skits for camp myself so they would be "impressive," and had them choreographed by my first counselor who was an expert dance instructor. Our Nights of Excellence were just that–excellent–and each one had to be a little bit more extravagant than the last one.

One particular Night of Excellence had begun with a wonderful idea and theme. We were going to have an Oscar Night complete with photos, long gowns, a red carpet, escorts, dinner, master of ceremonies, entertainment, Oscar winners and, of course, elaborate decorations. We had spent weeks with the young women preparing invitations, rounding up formal attire for each girl, practicing the entertainment, coaxing the young men to be escorts, purchasing food, ironing tablecloths and a myriad of other "essential" tasks that would make this an evening to remember. Despite the fact I had a cast on my arm from breaking my wrist while roller-skating with the youth two weeks earlier, I was looking forward to the excitement.

On the night of the event, as I was racing around the house barking orders at my family while they made several trips to the car with more decorations, my husband stopped for a moment and posed a simple question. In his calm and sensible manner he asked, "Dear, does this event really need to be this much of a production?" I paused, while holding twelve strands of Christmas lights in my arms, then responded in a high-pitched squeal, "I don't know, but I don't have time to analyze it right now! I have to get these fichus trees to the cultural hall so we can put the twinkly lights on them!" I then dashed to the church at the speed of sound, transformed the gym into the Kodak Theater of Hollywood, donned my glamorous dress and wiped the smudged mascara from under my eyes just in time to greet the arriving guests with a warm and inviting smile. It was indeed an exciting occasion and we received much praise from the girls, parents and stake Young Women Leaders. And no one was able to tell that I had a splitting headache and was feeling slightly nauseous.

Later, when I actually made time to analyze the situation—and several others like it—I realized I had to be careful of my intentions when "magnifying" my calling. Was I spending more time and energy on making the occasion perfect, or in helping the girls and other leaders realize their potential in becoming perfected? And along the way, what kind of example was I setting for my family? If service in the church was turning me into Momzilla, I probably wasn't doing it right.

The example of Mary and Martha came to mind. Martha was "cumbered about much serving" and was "careful and troubled about many things" (Luke 10:40-41). While taking care of duties is necessary and taking extra care to do them with perfection is admirable, we would do well to keep a balance with our perfectionist tendencies and remember that "one thing is needful" and to choose "that good part" (Luke 10: 42).

Great Expectations

For some perfectionists, the expectations are not only high for themselves but also for others around them. Brad, for instance, (a fictional character, but someone you may recognize) often becomes angry and frustrated when others around him don't perform as he thinks they should. He believes there is one proper way of doing things and everyone around him should conform. After all, his way is more efficient.

It seems that every day Brad has to lecture some employee or family member for their failure to meet his expectations.

One particular week caused Brad to be especially frustrated. A niece and nephew had come to visit and spend time with their cousins who were similar in age. They weren't disobedient or contrary; they just didn't seem to keep their belongings in the right place. Brad had asked them to stack their belongings in the corner of the bedroom. He had even demonstrated for them so there would be no confusion. He also had instructed them on how to wind the hose after they had used it for running through the sprinklers.

One afternoon, Brad drove into the driveway and almost ran over the garden hose. He immediately stormed into the house and yelled for the kids. "How many times have I told you to put that hose back where you found it! Just forget running through the sprinklers the rest of the week!" When the children apologized and started to retrieve the hose, Brad snapped, "Don't bother! I'll do it myself. Then I'll know it will be done right."

Brad's perfection creates conflicts in his relationships. His employees resent having to comply with his "routine," and his family members avoid him out of fear of ridicule. Brad would like to have a better relationship with his family, but it seems they don't listen and they make excuses for their failures. Therefore, he often finds it easier to avoid close relationships altogether. Having this myopic view and irrational expectations for others, robs an individual of the greater vision and joy that could take place.

I recall one Sunday as I sat in sacrament meeting. The sacrament prayer had been given and the bread was being passed. Our youngest son, who was a deacon at the time, was dressed in his white shirt and tie and was fulfilling his priesthood duty. I had just recently purchased him a pair of new dress pants that would be appropriate for church. The weather was becoming warmer now and I had decided he needed pants in a lighter weight and color. I hadn't yet altered them to fit properly over his shoes with a hemmed slit in the side, and last I had noticed, they were still waiting patiently on the sewing machine.

As the deacons walked reverently down the aisles, I happened to glance at the unexpected sight of the pants being worn by my son. Because I had a meeting prior to this one, I had not seen what he was wearing before he left the house. But there he was, for all the ward to see, in his pants that were not only too long, but had been self-altered by what appeared to be a dull pocket knife! I was mortified! And for the next forty-five minutes, the only thing on my mind was the sight of those embarrassing pants! I could envision all the little proper ladies in the ward pursing their lips, rolling their eyes and turning an accusing look my way. "How could she possibly allow her son to enter the chapel dressed like that! It looks as if a piranha attacked his pant leg! She should have more parental control. The next thing you know, he'll be skipping church, hiding across the street in the baseball dugouts and smoking Marlboros!"

I had been humiliated by an overzealous 12-year-old who didn't have the patience or good sense to wait for his mother to properly alter his trousers. These were expensive pants. They were made of very fine fabric, and now they were ruined! What could he have been thinking? I seethed through the rest of the meeting.

Luckily, I had two more hours of simmering before the attack on my son could begin. By then, the seething had decreased to a small twitch at my eye and I was able to calm myself just enough to call upon my well-rehearsed counseling skills. "Son, what was your understanding of the method we would use to alter your pants?" He responded with bright eyes and a lilt in his voice, "Oh, I knew how busy you had been this week and I could see you wouldn't have time to fix my pants, so I fixed them myself! It was easy, I just cut a slit on each side and it worked out just fine. They fit over my shoes just how I like them. Cool, huh?"

"Cool." That's all that came out. Just "cool." In his mind, he had been thoughtful of my time constraints and had done me a favor. He felt pride in his accomplishment of doing the job himself. More importantly, he had gotten himself to church and was prepared and worthy to honor his priesthood by assisting in the holy ordinance of the sacrament. And I almost missed it! Because of my preoccupation with his frayed and unsightly pants, I missed the opportunity to properly worship during the sacrament and I almost missed the chance to see the larger vision. Having frayed pants was a lot better than having frayed nerves. It certainly wasn't going to keep him out of the Celestial Kingdom. But if I continued to focus on this kind of perfection rather than working toward perfection, it could certainly do harm to my salvation.

I never "re-did" the pants. It was a good reminder for me each time I watched him pass the sacrament that there was a higher purpose. The eye twitching eventually went away, and in spite of the ladies with the pursed lips, I could worship in peace and joy.

Double-Edged Sword

Striving for perfection is a double-edged sword because it often springs from a desire to perform well, look our best or be first place. The problem is not in taking pride in our work, having high standards or reaching for the prize. The problems begin with the emotional consequences of not performing well. Many suffer from heightened feelings of guilt, humiliation, tension, frustration, disappointment or anger. Despite their best efforts, they still feel as if they don't measure-up, they'll never get things right, they won't ever be able to please and they will never be accepted. Perfectionism becomes a problem when it causes physical and emotional wear or when fear of mistakes keeps a person from accomplishing his goals, taking risks, feeling happiness or enjoying relationships.

The pursuit of perfection and the accompanying inability to achieve it can evolve into other, more complicated issues. Depression and anxiety disorders often result from perfectionist attitudes. Being perfect consistently is consistently impossible. The whole belief system is irrational and unrealistic.

As a high school counselor, I encountered young people with eating disorders such as anorexia nervosa and bulimia who held some perfectionist beliefs. Often they suffered from these disorders because of real or perceived messages of inadequacy. They might have been told by a friend that they are too fat. They might have been complimented for an athletic performance, then given instruction on how to do even better the next time. Perhaps they were praised by a parent for their good grades, then told they needed to raise the one B to an A. They absorbed these messages differently than most and things became confusing and out of control for them. In order to take charge and regain some control, starving or purging seemed to be the answer.

Sometimes it is difficult to distinguish the rather thin line between striving for perfection and perfectionism. Elder Cecil O. Samuelson gives these helpful contrasts:

Doing Your Best

You desire to give things your best efforts and are satisfied when you do.

You know it's okay if you make a mistake. You move on and see your mistake as an opportunity for growth and learning.

You want to do your personal best and you try not to compare your achievements with those of others. You don't need to be the best at all things.

You can find joy in doing the things you love, and you can get things accomplished.

Trying to do your best and perfecting yourself "line upon line" with the Savior's help is Christ-centered because you need the Atonement.

Perfectionism

You have a list of "shoulds" and "have to's" and are dissatisfied even if you complete them.

Mistakes bring feelings of self-hatred. You don't want to do anything because you are afraid of failure.

You feel tremendous pressure to earn others' approval. You must be the best or "perfect" in your tasks.

Your need to do things perfectly leads to procrastination until you have time to do it "perfectly," and you feel driven by fear or duty instead of love.

Perfectionism is self-centered. You measure yourself against your own standards and against others' standards, not God's.

("What Does It Mean to Be Perfect?" *New Era*, Jan. 2006, 10-13)

Those who have perfectionist tendencies find it difficult to remember that "lengthening your stride" gets you further than performing the splits, and that "reaching for the stars" does not necessitate becoming one.

When our oldest son was about six years old, he did something that required a disciplinary consequence. For the life of me, I cannot remember what the deed was, but I remember what followed quite vividly. We discussed what the punishment would be. I knew from past experience that he would suggest a stiffer penalty than I would. This made my parenting job much easier considering the fact that I could lessen the penalty and therefore look as if I were "the good guy." True to form, he announced his harsh sentence through quivering lips.

I shook my head in disbelief and wondered if we were talking about the same misdeeds. I negotiated a counter offer. He bowed his head in resignation and accepted the offer. Later, as we discussed the situation, my already tender heart practically burst as he sputtered discouragingly, "I wanted to be perfect like Joseph Smith, and now I'm not." I hugged him and explained that Joseph Smith wasn't perfect either. I followed up with some quick, "motherly" advice.

Years have gone by and he is a father of his own young sons. If a similar situation happens, and it probably will, I hope he will say something much more profound than I did. I hope he can explain to his sons as Elder Joseph B. Wirthlin did, "Except for the Lord, we have all made mistakes. The question is not whether we will trip and fall, but rather, how will we respond?.... Do you not know that the Church is a place for imperfect people to gather together—even with all their mortal frailties—and become better? ...I am not aware of any sign on the door of our meetinghouses that reads "Restricted Entrance—Perfect People Only" ("Concern for the One" *Ensign*, May 2008, 19).

The Great Pretender

Fear of judgment can be devastating to those who are suffering from perfectionism. We think our children suffer from peer pressure, but examine how we as adults hide our situations rather than seeking help for them. We also rescue our children rather than allowing them to take the natural consequences for their actions. All this because we don't want the neighbors to think that we are incapable or that our children might be flawed.

Our highly competitive American culture often promotes this perception of perfection. Even those who appear outwardly to be successful, often suffer from inner experiences of value conflict and insecurity, striving by any means to protect their image. The process of putting on "masks" for appearance sake is exhausting and crippling. There is a great amount of energy in maintaining the facade. Creativity and individuality are often sacrificed in the constant search for peer validation. The cost is high, not only in dollars, but also in self-actualization and the development of one's full potential.

One only needs to talk with an adolescent trying to "fit in" with the rest of the crowd to see how the process begins. Personal inadequacy and rejection are common themes and the dynamics involved in hiding these from peers is phenomenal. There are academy award winning performances at every school and mall, and admission is free.

We could possibly excuse these youngsters as being immature and suggest that at some point in their lives they will recognize their true selves and be comfortable with who they are. However, if that same quest is still continuing when we are adults raising our own adolescents, we have a bigger problem than a bad case of acne.

I like how Phil McGraw described it in his book, *Life Strategies*. "As a society, we are losing it. When it comes to managing our own emotional lives, and training our children how to manage theirs, we're out of control but desperately pretending otherwise. We project an outward image of 'I'm alright. I can take it. I'll be okay,' because we fear judgment. Well it's not okay, and we'd better start changing... ...people with real problems hide them rather than seeking support, and those who don't sometimes wish they had after the doses of guilt, judgment, or alienation they received. We hide problems, and judge those who don't or can't hide theirs. It's not working people–not even close."

I recall on more than one occasion calling a parent from the counseling office to express my concern for their child who exhibited behaviors related to substance abuse. I offered some suggestions as to how they might proceed with gaining more information to evaluate the problem and options to consider. Too often, the information was denied or disregarded. I recognize the difficulty in admitting a problem such as this either in our children or in ourselves. We are frightened of judgment. We assume that our community or church members will discover our imperfections, judge our parenting, or gossip about our family. Unfortunately, many times we are right in our assumptions.

Here again, in order for us to heal physically and spiritually, and to assist our families to do the same, we must first admit our imperfections. That act alone, can free us to take the necessary steps that will enable us to recover from the "lumps" and find our way smoothly to finding joy and health. We can more fully allow the atonement to operate in our lives. By the same token, we should not act too quickly to condemn others who find themselves in difficult situations. We are not the judge and jury. As Moroni stated: "Condemn me not because of mine imperfection, neither my father, because of his imperfection, neither them who have written before him; but rather give thanks unto God that he hath made manifest unto you our imperfections, that ye may learn to be more wise than we have been" (Mormon 9:31).

We would do well to remember what Neal A. Maxwell taught: "the Church is 'for the perfecting of the saints' (Eph. 4:12); it is not a well-provisioned rest home for the already perfected" ("A Brother Offended" *Ensign,* May 1982, 37).

2

A Guilt Trip Is
No Vacation

Guilt in its purest form is probably a good thing. It's that feeling of remorse that you get when you're five years old and you steal something from the grocery store. It's your conscience telling you that this was a bad idea, and when your father finds out, the idea will seem even worse.

Something strange happens to guilt as people get a little older. For some, it goes away altogether leaving them in a superficial state of sinful bliss. For others, it seems to manifest itself into a Joan of Arc-like martyrdom. It becomes a highly contagious disease that allows the "victim" to embark upon guilt trips of many forms. It seems as if the more trips the victim takes, the more the journey is "enjoyed." The host or hostess invites others to come to the party. And no party is complete without refreshments–such as entire family size bags of potato chips followed by a side stack of Double-Stuffed Oreos.

The above description is only slightly embellished. Guilt can actually be a gift of saving grace, or a self-destructive trap. Here is where that "without bruising yourself" part comes into play. While guilt is a necessary and appropriate prerequisite to purification, some choose to suffer from guilt long after any reasonable amount of time or without reason. Some even use guilt as a manipulation strategy.

I suppose most parents have trumped their children with the guilt trip card from time to time. We coerce our children into responding positively to our requests by causing them to believe we will suffer tremendously if they do not. I was even presented with a humorous Mother's Day card from one of my children with the message on the front that read, "Better Parenting Through Guilt." When opened, there was a cheery audio voice that said, "In motherhood, no tool is more effective than skillfully administered guilt. Anything you want is within your reach with simple phrases like, 'Don't worry about me. I'm fine,' or how about, 'Well, if it will make you happy,' or in extreme cases, 'Well, I guess I have to blame myself.' So the next time you feel like you're losing control, why not try guilt." On the inside the written message was, "It's Mother's Day. Lay it on thick!" My darling child wrote a quick P.S. indicating that I wasn't guilty of using this tactic and that I was the best mother ever. (I think they will be running for a political office soon.) I did read that Elder Steven E. Snow mentioned that his mother was a "travel agent for guilt trips," and he seems to have turned out just fine.

However, manipulation with guilt can be destructive when used as a device to blame, control, or threaten. The person administering the guilt is often a master of deception and is skilled in creating situations that encourage the "receiver" to do things their way, even when it goes against the "receiver's" better judgment or moral code. Consider how a young man manipulates a young woman by asking her why she won't "prove" her love to him, or if he accuses her of cheating on him if she talks with another boy, or if he makes her feel guilty for having fun with other people while he is "suffering" in some way.

Some people feign illnesses or hardships to arouse our sense of guilt or take advantage of our help so we will take over tasks that they could do. Some may threaten negative consequences for themselves if we don't respond to their request. Phrases like, "I'll fail this class and not graduate if you don't do this homework for me. You don't want that do you?" or "I'll have to go to jail if you tell someone. It will be all your fault." Situations such as these are manipulation strategies that cause the "receiver" to believe their alternatives are limited to choices with the least sense of guilt.

Irrational Beliefs

The dictionary defines the word "guilt" as a "feeling of responsibility or remorse for some offense, crime, wrong, etc., whether real or imagined." It is often described as a conscience, an inherent human trait. It can become a motivator for change, or an obstacle that immobilizes and interferes with a healthy life.

There can be many irrational beliefs that lie in the shadows of guilt. Some choose to suffer from guilt over events for which they have no control. There have been many events in our world as of late with hurricanes, tornadoes, tsunamis, floods, fires, earthquakes and more. Many people have died, lost their homes, or become orphaned. Starvation and disease permeate the land. Some feel guilt over not being able to cure everyone or save all those who suffer. Some feel guilt because they have had a safe and peaceful life in contrast to those whose lives have been devastated.

Many missionaries have been sent to countries which have been ravaged by war, where food, shelter and medical aid is in short supply for its citizens, or where poverty and lack of hope seem to be the menu of the day. When they return home, they do so carrying a large dose of guilt. They return and enter a house with many rooms, air conditioning, cupboards and refrigerators full of food and a bedroom with a comfortable bed. Consequently, they sometimes feel guilt for what they have and others have not. This type of guilt can become an avenue for self-imposed punishment.

Sheri Dew mentioned some of those same feelings upon her return from international experiences. One particular trip affected her deeply. "Maybe it was seeing so much poverty. Maybe it was meeting so many children orphaned by war. Maybe it was all the people I'd seen who seemed to have no hope. Maybe it was all of the above.

"During the long flight, with lots of time to think, I found myself vacillating between gratitude and guilt–gratitude for all I had and guilt because of all I had" ...(*No One Can Take Your Place, 176*).

There are those who carry guilt upon the death of a loved one or because of a divorce of a family member. Some feel guilt because of an illness that does not allow them to serve their family in the way they would like. Many parents feel guilty for the negative choices that their children make. To assume we are totally, irrevocably responsible for all the natural disasters, choices of others, illnesses and deaths is totally and irrevocably irrational. This does not mean that we cannot do our part. It does help, however, to recognize that we are the only ones we can control, and by doing so, we can positively affect the lives of others. But we cannot control them or the situations in which they find themselves.

While this may seem insensitive, consider the alternative of allowing guilt to fester and destroy our health and relationships. Rather than be immobilized because of natural disasters and the conditions in the world, certain that one person cannot make a difference, remember the words of Mother Teresa, "If you can't feed a hundred people, then feed just one...We ourselves feel that what we are doing is just a drop in the ocean. But the ocean would be less because of that missing drop."

Rather than giving up on yourself for your assumed failure as a parent, consider this insight. "The guilt they (parents) feel centers on a common but inaccurate conclusion. They assume that their children's problems provide *prima facie* evidence of their failure. 'We must have done something wrong, or our kids wouldn't have these problems.' Wrong! By this standard Adam and Eve were failures as parents. After all, one son murdered another. Lehi and Sariah must have also been failures since several of their children were rebellious and exceptionally wicked. Even our eternal parents fail by this standard. As perfect as they are, one third of their children contradicted their will and were forever cast out" (see Revelation 12:4) (Taylor, Gary D., *Life is Easy, I Just Decide It's Hard*, 9).

We must set aside those things over which we have no control and concentrate on doing what we can with our abilities, time, means and talents, being careful to "see that all these things are done in wisdom and order; for it is not requisite that a man should run faster than he has strength..." (Mosiah 4:27).

Some choose to suffer from guilt even after they have been forgiven. Linda, a character in the Book of Mormon Video Presentations, is helped by her bishop to understand this concept. As she looks at a portrait of Jesus which hangs on his wall, she indicates to the bishop that, "After the things I've done wrong, He wouldn't want me as one of His children." The bishop asks her to look at the picture one more time and to continue looking at it until they both see the same thing. Then he gives her this important message to dispel her irrational beliefs, "If I understand you correctly, you see someone who is so good that He wouldn't want you to be one of His daughters. I want you to see the person I know. I see someone who is so good, so full of mercy and wants you to be one of His daughters so much, that He was willing to suffer and die so you could repent and be forgiven. Can you see that person?" ("Becoming Children of Christ").

Elder Richard G. Scott gave this encouragement, "To you who have sincerely repented yet continue to feel the burden of guilt, realize that to continue to suffer for sins when there has been proper repentance and forgiveness of the Lord is prompted by the master of deceit. Lucifer will encourage you to continue to relive the details of past mistakes, knowing that such thoughts can hamper your progress. Thus he attempts to tie the strings to the mind and body so that he can manipulate you like a puppet to discourage personal achievement" ("Peace of Conscience and Peace of Mind," *Ensign*, Nov. 2004, 16).

To determine if the guilt we feel is unhealthy and irrational, we can use the following guidelines posed by clinical psychologist, Gary G. Taylor:

1. Do I feel guilty about a sin I have done my best to forsake?
2. Do I feel guilty about something that I cannot directly control?
3. Do I feel guilty about a mistake or shortcoming that is just part of the human condition?
4. Do I feel guilty about a mistake or shortcoming that isn't a moral issue?
5. Is the guilt I feel moving me closer to or further away from Christ? (*Life is Easy, I Just Decide It's Hard*, 13).

Guilt as an Obstacle

This story of the iron wedge is an example of how damaging guilt can be if left unattended.

"The ice storm wasn't generally destructive. True, a few wires came down and there was a sudden jump in accidents along the highway. Walking out of doors became unpleasant and difficult. It was disagreeable weather, but it was not serious. Normally, the big walnut tree could easily have borne the weight that formed on its spreading limbs. It was the iron wedge in its heart that caused the damage.

"The story of the iron wedge began years ago when the white-haired farmer was a lad on his father's homestead. The sawmill had then only recently been moved from the valley, and the settlers were still finding tools and odd pieces of equipment scattered about...

"On this particular day, it was a faller's wedge–wide, flat, and heavy, a foot or more long, and splayed from mighty poundings. The path from the south pasture did not pass the woodshed; and, because he was already late for dinner, the lad laid the wedge...between the limbs of the young walnut tree his father had planted near the front gate. He would take the wedge to the shed right after dinner, or sometime when he was going that way.

"He truly meant to, but he never did. It was there between the limbs, a little tight, when he attained his manhood. It was there, now firmly gripped, when he married and took over his father's farm. It was half grown over on the day the threshing crew ate dinner under the tree. ... Grown in and healed over, the wedge was still in the tree the winter the ice storm came.

"In the chill silence of that wintry night, with the mist like rain sifting down and freezing where it fell, one of the three major limbs split away from the trunk and crashed to the ground. This so unbalanced the remainder of the top that it, too, split apart and went down. When the storm was over, not a twig of the once-proud tree remained.

"Early the next morning, the farmer went out to mourn his loss. 'Wouldn't have had that happen for a thousand dollars,' he said. 'Prettiest tree in the valley, that was.'

"Then his eyes caught sight of something in the splintered ruin. 'The wedge,' he muttered reproachfully. 'The wedge I found in the south pasture.' A glance told him why the tree had fallen. Growing edge-up in the trunk, the wedge had prevented the limb fibers from knitting together as they should" (Samuel T. Whitman, "Forgotten Wedges," quoted by Spencer W. Kimball, in Conference Report, Apr. 1966, 70-71).

The wedge stands as a symbol of guilt. It could be a feeling of shame for having mistreated someone who has now passed on. It could be a feeling of responsibility for negative circumstances that have befallen a loved one. It could be a feeling of regret for not pleasing someone or everyone. It could be feelings of remorse for sins of commission or omission. Whatever our personal "wedge" consists of, we, like the tree will be weakened and eventually collapse if the guilt we feel is not acted upon, lifted up and carried away. The wedge in the tree prevented it from growing and developing properly. Likewise, we will be inhibited from progressing if the guilt we carry is allowed to be a burden rather than a motivator for change.

My father recently told me of an incident involving my grandmother. She lived with my parents for many years after she was widowed and her children were grown. I remember her in our home while I was a teenager. She told us when our dresses were too short, reminded us of our chores, gathered vegetables from the garden in her apron, and crocheted hundreds of doilies. She was generous with her meager earnings, sharing food or a piece of jewelry or some treasure with her grandchildren who visited. She was the matriarch of all family reunions and lived to be one hundred years old. I admired her strength, living most of her life without the companionship of her husband.

As the story goes, when my grandmother was eighty years old, she sat rather despondent in a chair one day. When my father approached her, she said, "Go down and fetch the bishop. He needs to come here right now." She had no intention of waiting until church on Sunday or of calling for an appointment. She needed to see the bishop immediately! There was definitely something on her mind. My father obediently walked down the short road to the bishop's home and requested a meeting. The bishop kindly accompanied him back to the house where my grandmother continued to sit in her chair. He gently took her hand and asked her what she wanted to discuss. She then tearfully explained to him of a wrong-doing that took place sixty years earlier.

My poor grandmother had buried the "wedge" deeply attempting to dismiss it and grow around it, but it had remained a burden she alone carried with her all of those years. Like an albatross around her neck, it weighed heavily upon her soul and caused her great sorrow. With all the other hardships she had to endure, this one could have been lifted years before. She could have felt the redeeming power of repentance and thus had more peace. At least now, the bishop could reassure her that a loving Savior had atoned for her sin and that he was certain that the life she had led for all the years since had proven to the Lord that she was worthy of His forgiveness. Her anguish left as she yielded to the Judge of Israel and to her Savior for a remission of her sins. What a relief from a bitter sorrow she had endured for so long!

"How difficult it must be for Jesus Christ, our Savior and Redeemer, to see so many needlessly suffer, because His gift of repentance is ignored. It must pain Him deeply to see the pointless agony both in this life and beyond the veil that accompany the unrepented sinner after all He did so that we need not suffer" (Richard G. Scott, "The Path to Peace and Joy," *Ensign*, Nov 2000, 27).

Unattended guilt, like the unattended wedge, can cause us to split from the trunk and crash to the ground. Over time, it causes many irrational thoughts and therefore irrational deeds. It may make a person overly sensitive to any implication of wrong on his part and cause him to become obsessed with always being right. It may cause others to deny themselves joy and happiness because of the irrational belief that they don't deserve it. Some may be "overly generous" with their time or material belongings unaware that guilt is the motivating factor for their behavior. Some may be overly responsible for everything in an attempt to make everyone comfortable and happy while ignoring their own desires and needs. Still others may become so immobilized by fear of doing, acting or saying the wrong thing that they choose inactivity, alcohol and other drugs, or large doses of food for temporary comfort.

Guilt as a Motivation for Change

Guilt can be a useful tool in directing our moral compass. When our conscience is bothered, it allows us to make judgments about what is right and what is wrong. It can prevent us from acting in negative ways. It prevents conflicts, and contributes to more positive relationships. It allows us to act appropriately and eliminate actions that we might regret later.

Guilt also becomes an asset when it brings to our remembrance situations in our conduct that require change. We feel regret or sorrow and take the appropriate actions to make amends and be forgiven. A clear conscience provides calm and peace and allows us to cope with adversity. Charlotte Bronte says of this type of guilt, "If all the world hated you, and believed you wicked, while your own conscience approved you, and absolved you from guilt, you would not be without friends."

It is impossible to mention guilt as a motivator for change without recognizing the atonement. What a wonderful, peaceful message it is that we are all invited to come unto the Savior and be saved from the torment of guilt. "Behold, I have come unto the world to bring redemption unto the world, to save the world from sin. Therefore, whoso repenteth and cometh unto me as a little child, him will I receive, for of such is the kingdom of God. Behold, for such I have laid down my life, and have taken it up again; therefore repent, and come unto me ye ends of the earth, and be saved" (3 Nephi 9:21-22).

In his epistle to the Philippians, Paul alludes to the change he has made when he remarks: "Brethren, I count not myself to have apprehended: but this one thing I do, forgetting those things which are behind, and reaching forth unto those things which are before, I press toward the mark for the prize of the high calling of God in Christ Jesus" (Philippians 3:13-14). John adds this message, "If we confess our sins, he is faithful and just to forgive us our sins and to cleanse us from all unrighteousness" (1 John 1:9).

The Book of Mormon is replete with examples of this power. After "mighty prayer and supplication" for his soul, Enos heard a voice that said, "Enos, thy sins are forgiven thee, and thou shalt be blessed. And I, Enos, knew that God could not lie; wherefore, my guilt was swept away" (Enos1:4-6). And almost immediately, he was able to turn his attention away from himself and toward serving his fellow man, "...my soul did rest... and I, Enos, went about among the people of Nephi, prophesying of things to come, and testifying of the things which I had heard and seen" (Enos 1:17,19). How sad it would have been, not only for Enos, but for many of the Nephites, had he allowed guilt of sin to be a barrier to his progress. Instead, with renewed peace in his heart, he was able to serve others as well.

Alma was also "racked with torment" with the memories of his sins and the guilt that he felt. "Yea, I did remember all my sins and iniquities, for which I was tormented with the pains of hell..." (Alma 36:12-13). Imagine suffering through a lifetime with such crippling feelings of hopelessness. But this would not only have affected Alma, it would have continued to be an example and a burden for his sons. Instead,

Alma recognized that he needed to put off his guilt in order to serve his family and others. As he considered the mercy of his Savior Jesus Christ, he was able to "remember my pains no more; yea, I was harrowed up by the memory of my sins no more. And oh, what joy, and what marvelous light I did behold; yea, my soul was filled with joy as exceeding as was my pain!

"Yea, I say unto you, my son, that there could be nothing so exquisite and so bitter as were my pains. Yea, and again I say unto you, my son, that on the other hand, there can be nothing so exquisite and sweet as was my joy."

Our daughter recognized the "sweet joy" that comes from having a second chance. She is talented in music as a vocalist, pianist and flutist. During high school, she qualified for the state competition in flute her first three years. The state competition was approaching for her final time as a senior. She had practiced more intensely than ever before and felt prepared for the qualifying event. The day arrived and it was her turn to stand and face the judge. She was confident but filled with the nervousness that competition and scrutiny can bring. She began her piece and all was going well. Then, she made an error. She also noticed the judge look down at her score sheet and begin to write. Losing her concentration, she made another error. She finished the piece and left the room. I thought it sounded lovely and was ready to congratulate her but I could tell by her eyes she was not pleased with her performance. I neither have the talent of a flutist nor a trained ear of a judge, but I can read my daughter's expression. She looked down at her feet and simply said, "I'll meet you at home."

When she did arrive home, she allowed the tears to fall. She knew she would not be going to the state competition. It was disappointing, even heartbreaking. She knew that if she had only been given a second chance to prove herself, she would have been able to show she was worthy of the state competition. However, in talking with her, she said she was okay with how things had transpired. She would have liked to go state, but she had realized an even more important lesson. Although she had only one chance to prove her musical talent in that forum, she recognized that she always had a second chance when it came to the atonement. The sorrow that she felt over the loss of this opportunity, paled in comparison to the anguish she would feel if she never had a second chance to prove herself to her Heavenly Father. That feeling presented such a powerful testimony to her, that it prompted the composition of a song with the following lyrics:

How can I find
Some peace of mind
When I'm put to the test
And fail to do my best?
How can I pursue
What I hope to do
When I stumble and fall
Even though I give my all?

"Dear child," He answers my call.
"I'll lift you up when you fall.
This is my gift to you. It's what I came to do.
Fear departs when faith endures."

How can a man with a lifetime of sin
Ever hope to find the light from within?
How can a woman with her share of sorrow
Find through her hopelessness a better tomorrow?

"Dear child," He answers their call.
"I'll lift you up when you fall.
This is my gift to you. It's what I came to do.
Fear departs when faith endures."

Is there a hope for a brighter day
For one such as I?
And I call to Him for comfort and joy
That I may know His way.

"Dear child," He answers our call.
I'll lift you up when you fall.
This is my gift to you. It's what I came to do.
Fear departs when faith endures."

3

TERRIBLE, HORRIBLE, NO GOOD AND VERY BAD

A favorite book among children, and many adults, is Judith Viorst's book titled *Alexander and the Terrible, Horrible, No Good, Very Bad Day*. Alexander is a young boy with seemingly more trials than any human should have to encounter. He is disgruntled by the fact that the gum he was chewing at bedtime is caked in his hair by morning. He is disgusted by the fact that he doesn't get a window seat on his ride to school. He is angry with his teacher who doesn't like the drawing of his invisible castle. To add to his misery, the dentist tells him he has a cavity, there is no dessert in his lunch, his mother prepared lima beans for dinner and he has to wear his railroad train pajamas to bed. His response to these events is to tell everyone that he might as well move to Australia. The book closes with his mother's assurance that everyone has bad days, even people who live in Australia. This realization allows him to sleep peacefully, even in his railroad train pajamas.

Although this book is intended to delight young readers, there is much that can be gleaned from examining Alexander's approach to opposition: 1) Being negative about his situation did nothing to change it. 2) His negativity did nothing to improve his life or the lives of his friends and family. 3) He made a choice to be negative and it continued to be a habit. 4) When he changed his attitude and perceptions, he felt more peace. By making these comparisons, we can come to realize how often we might engage in negativity, and how futile it is to do so.

Opposition in All Things

Opposition is a significant attribute of mortal life. Modern revelation tells us: "...it must needs be that the devil should tempt the children of men, or they could not be agents unto themselves; for if they never should have bitter they could not know the sweet" (D&C 29:39.)

Eldred G. Smith further explains, "Some of us think we have the bitter and not enough of the sweet. This is normal. We all have our trials of life to strengthen us. Each thinks he has the hardest or most severe trials. It may be that they are the most difficult only because they are the hardest or most difficult for you. The diamond is enhanced and made more valuable with polishing. Steel is made harder and more valuable through tempering. So also opposition builds the character of man" ("Opposition in Order to Strengthen Us" *Ensign*, Jan. 1974, 62).

It is important to recognize that not only will we experience opposition, but that it is an integral part of the complex fabric of life. Happiness and joy are not alternatives to opposition, they are the results of coping with opposition in a positive and healthy way. No amount of negative behavior was going to change Alexander's circumstances. The opposition would still exist. So it is in our lives. Disgruntled, disdainful, negative attitudes about challenges, difficulties, or obstacles will have no power in removing them.

When we see a patch of thorns in our way, we should not be like Alexander and decide there is no way through it, nag about the improper way the garden was managed, curse God because of the lack of rain, and complain to all our friends. We can recognize it as a negative situation which calls for positive thinking. We can take action and use a pitchfork to remove the patch. We can smooth the ground and plant seeds for flowers, and in the process, grow ourselves.

Notice that being positive about the thorns does not constitute ignoring their dangers. Walking through them with a Pollyanna-like smile, while commenting that your puncture wounds "aren't that bad and don't hurt at all," is also not productive. Some assume that being positive about obstacles means to suppress the grief and disappointment, put on a happy face and pretend they aren't there. There is as much danger in that solution as there is to constant wallowing. Nothing is learned, no decision is made and no action is taken.

I remember hearing a woman comment about her 25-year marriage to her husband and remarking that they had never had a fight. Did she mean that she never disagreed with her husband? I decided that perhaps she had meant a loud, nasty, yelling, type of fight. Still, I was a bit concerned that one of the partners had succumbed to pernicious martyrdom. How does a relationship grow and flourish if one or both of the partners allows conflict to be brushed under the table and shoved into the corner? Avoiding negative information and being resistant to finding solutions are destructive. Being positive and hopeful while forging ahead to find solutions to problems is not the same as exhibiting superficial, pretentious cheerfulness.

As a society, I believe we are teaching our children some inconsistent concepts. In an attempt NOT to be negative, we are hindering our children's opportunity to learn from opposition. We try to squelch anything that might be painful, conflicting or disappointing to them. In a newspaper article recently, I noticed that a town of suburban parents decided that they would not choose all-stars from the regular league baseball teams to play in a post-season tournament. The reason for the decision was that they didn't want anyone to think they were better than anyone else and have ill feelings over the choices. The article was titled, "Hurrah for Mediocrity." While I do believe that some competitions have become over dramatized, I also feel concern over our desire to shelter our children from conflict or disappointment when they might be able to learn so much from experiencing it. Wouldn't they be better served by being taught how to be a good sport whether or not they were chosen for the team? And how about making goals to train for a more improved season next year? These attributes are only acquired from wise adults who help build character and strength in children by teaching them strategies to cope with opposition. What happens later when the mission or the job or the marriage has conflict?

When the Prophet Joseph Smith was a prisoner in the jail at Liberty, Missouri, the Lord encouraged him with these words: "...if thou shouldst be cast into the pit, or into the hands of murderers, and the sentence of death passed upon thee; if thou be cast into the deep; if the billowing surge conspire against thee; if fierce winds become thine enemy; if the heavens gather blackness, and all the elements combine to hedge up the way; and above all, if the very jaws of hell shall gape open the mouth wide after thee, know thou, my son, that all these things shall give thee experience, and shall be for thy good" (D&C 122:7).

Surely these words were a source of strength for the prophet. But it is the next section of the book that shows his resolve in finding a way through the thorns. Although he was incarcerated, he still took action to assist the saints and guide them with resources for changing their circumstances. He urged them to gather information about the sufferings and abuses they had encountered by the state, to list damages sustained, name those who had a hand in their oppressions, gather up libelous publications and present their information to the heads of government. (D&C 123) He impressed upon them that it was an imperative duty and that "a very large ship is benefited very much by a very small helm in the time of a storm, by being kept workways with the wind and the waves." He further guided his followers by saying, "Therefore, dearly beloved brethren, let us cheerfully do all things that lie in our power; and then may we stand still, with the utmost assurance, to see the salvation of God, and for his arm to be revealed" (D&C 123:16-17).

What a great definition for facing opposition! "Cheerfully do all things that lie in our power" and then rely on God.

Improve the Shining Moments

In Alexander's case, negativity did nothing to improve his life or the lives of his family and friends. That is true with each of us as well. Part of our purpose here on the earth is to prove and improve ourselves and then continue to serve our fellow man. Sometimes that means to do whatever is in our power to call upon the positive aspects of our lives in spite of life's difficulties.

You may have heard the story of the carpenter that was hired to help a neighbor restore an old farmhouse. He had just finished a rough first day on the job. A flat tire made him lose an hour of work, his electric saw quit, and then his old pickup refused to start.

While his neighbor drove him home, he sat in stony silence. On arriving, he invited the neighbor in to meet his family. As they walked toward the front door, he paused briefly at a small tree, touching the tips of the branches with both hands. When opening the door, he underwent an amazing transformation. His tanned face was wreathed in smiles and he hugged his two small children and gave his wife a kiss.

Afterward, he walked the neighbor to the car. They passed the tree and the neighbor's curiosity got the better of him. He asked him about what he had seen him do earlier. "Oh, that's my trouble tree," he replied. "I know I can't help having troubles on the job, but one thing's for sure, troubles don't belong in the house with my wife and children. So, I just hang them up on the tree every night when I come home. Then in the morning I pick them up again and take care of things."

"Funny thing is," he smiled, "when I come out in the morning to pick them up, there aren't nearly as many as I remember hanging up the night before."

Unfortunately, we often take out our frustrations upon those people we love the most. Perhaps it is because we know they will still love us in spite of our negative ways. But, if we have a duty to our fellow earthly travelers, and I believe we do, we must seek and share positive moments. The constant battery that pulses from negativity strains relationships, saps energy, and divides family members. Being positive also requires energy, but it attracts that same energy from others.

I have a plaque in my den that reads, "When Mom is not happy, ain't nobody happy." It is a reminder that one person's positive attitude or negative attitude can have a profound effect on the other members of the household. We don't have to allow a negative person to determine our mood, but it is certainly more difficult to maintain a cheerful heart with a constant message of gloom surrounding it. Negative people not only harm themselves, they alienate and harm the people in their home and community. Rather than making a positive contribution, they spread misery and infect others along the way. Being negative is contagious.

Consider the effects that someone like Alexander would have upon his family and friends if he continued his habits. He would soon discover that his brothers and several of his friends at school were starting to avoid him. That would fulfill his own prophesy that people are mean to him and he is disliked. He could become more rigid, close-minded and stuck in his own ways of interacting with others. His mother, usually cheerful and positive, could begin to feel defeated and become critical of all family members. As a result, his father would put up a protective barrier between himself and his wife, being silent for weeks at a time. Everyone would become locked in a vicious cycle of put-downs and name-calling. And Alexander would feel even more worthless and isolated.

While this is only speculation about the character of Alexander, it is a vivid and true example of how the disease of negativity spreads. It starts within small circles of family and friends, then extends to communities and nations. It is almost as if there is a predetermined destiny of suffering and everyone else is responsible for it. The belief system becomes, "I have been treated badly in the past and should expect nothing different in the future. No matter how much I extend my hand in friendship to others, I get slapped in return. I am what I am and nothing will ever change. I'm not being sincere if I act positively when I don't feel positive. I will always be disappointed if I believe in the good of others."

It is easy to find fault in others. It is a habit to complain. We are skilled at being our own worst critic. It is simple to allow a negative turn of events to color our view of the world. But none of these attitudes or behaviors will improve our life or the lives of our family. We will only miss out on the small joys that life brings. As Helen Keller stated, "No pessimist ever discovered the secrets of the stars or sailed to an uncharted land, or opened a new heaven to the human spirit."

Consider the many examples of Nephi as he exhibited a positive attitude, even in the face of constant negativity, complaining and criticism from his brothers. When Nephi and his brothers are asked to return to Jerusalem to obtain the plates of brass from Laban, Laman and Lemuel begin to murmur saying it would be too difficult. Nephi responds by saying, "I will go and do the things which the Lord hath commanded, for I know the Lord giveth no commandment unto the children of men, save he shall prepare a way for them that they may accomplish the thing which he commandeth them" (1 Nephi 3:7).

After Laman tries the first time to obtain the plates from Laban and is cast out of his house, the brothers decide to give up and return to the tent of their father. But Nephi, once again, seeks to be positive and chooses to find alternative ways to obtain the records. When the plan of trading gold and silver for the plates does not work, Laman becomes angry with Nephi. Lemuel follows Laman's example with harsh words and physical punishment toward their younger brothers. Even after an angel appears to them and assures them that Laban will be delivered into their hands, they still murmur. "How is it possible that the Lord will deliver Laban into our hands? Behold, he is a mighty man, and he can command fifty, yea even he can slay fifty; then why not us?" (1 Nephi 3:31).

Nephi's positive attitude and trust in the Lord continue to assist him and his family. He builds a new bow after his is broken in order to provide food for them. He builds a boat for them in which to cross the waters. Although his brothers continue to complain and call him a fool, he carries on as instructed.

We can vividly observe how the negativity of Laman and Lemuel caused heartache and pain for their family. In fact, many trials came upon the whole family because of their constant pessimism and disbelief. The same is true in our families and in our relationships with others. We can do much to create happiness, peace and contentment, or we can be a catalyst for turmoil and misery. President Spencer W. Kimball reminded us "that regardless of your present age, you are building your life;...it can be full of joy and happiness, or it can be full of misery. It all depends upon you and your attitudes, for you altitude, or the height you climb, is dependent upon your attitude or your response to situations" (*Ensign*, Nov. 1974, 80).

Negativity is a Habit and a Choice

Too often we have the habit of focusing on the negative side of those around us. It becomes easy to find fault, to criticize, to judge and then to openly complain. There is a lot of energy expended in choosing to be angry or resentful. While there are many situations we cannot control, we can control our day-to-day thoughts and attitudes. However, many small annoyances are viewed by some as giant problems. Our focus becomes out of balance. Petty, minor occurrences are blown out of proportion. It becomes a way of life and dictates our attitudes and actions.

I have seen friendships, even marriages dissolve when one or both partners choose to accumulate and store all that is negative until they become blind to what is positive about that relationship. They lose perspective. Rather than dealing with situations with humor, or forgiveness, or patience, they choose insensitivity, negativity and frustration. Instead of finding solutions, they find fault. Instead of being productive, they pout. Instead of being creative, they become critical.

This type of behavior is illustrated in the story of the "The Grapefruit Syndrome." "My husband and I had been married about two years when

I read an article recommending that married couples discuss truthfully and candidly the habits or mannerisms they find annoying in each other. The theory was that if partners knew of such annoyances, they could correct them before resentful feelings developed. It made sense to me. I talked with my husband about the idea. After some hesitation, he agreed to give it a try.

"As I recall, we were to name five things we found annoying. I started off. I remember only my first complaint: grapefruit. I told him I didn't like the way he ate grapefruit. Instead of cutting it open and eating it with a spoon, he peeled it and ate it a section at a time. Nobody else I knew ate grapefruit like that. Could I be expected to spend a lifetime, and even an eternity, watching my husband eat grapefruit like that? Although I have forgotten them, I'm sure my other complaints were of similar importance.

"Then it was his turn. It has been more than half a century, but I still carry a mental image of my husband's thoughtful, puzzled expression. He looked at me and said, 'I can't think of anything I don't like about you.'

"Gasp. I quickly turned my back, not knowing how to explain my tears. I had found fault with him over such trivial things, while he hadn't even noticed any of my peculiar and no doubt annoying habits. I wish I could say this experience completely cured me of faultfinding. It didn't. But it did teach me early in my marriage that we need to keep in perspective, and usually ignore, the small differences in our spouse's habits and personalities. Whenever I hear of married couples being incompatible, I always wonder if they are suffering from what I now call the grapefruit syndrome" (Lola B. Walters, "The Grapefruit Syndrome," *Liahona*, Sep. 1999, 24).

While finding fault with others can become a habit, so can choosing to find fault with oneself. Through negative self-talk we convince ourselves of all that is wrong with our bodies, our brains and our being. We can create a defeatist and pessimistic attitude. We grasp on to the most self-critical thoughts and allow our brain to record and replay at will. How we act and what we become is a product of those thoughts.

Our brains are often compared to computers. But unlike a computer which has fixed wiring and connections, our human brains can make changes in their operation. We can train ourselves to believe the positive about ourselves. We can silence the negative thoughts and acknowledge the positive ones. As Shirley MacLaine said, "Dwelling on the negative simply contributes to its power."

Although the lumps of life that often come to us are situations over which we have no control, we still have control over our attitude. We may not be able to control illnesses, but we can choose to be positive about the cure. We may not have control over product prices, but we can make positive choices about consumer spending. We may not have control over old age and its impending aches, but we don't have to be old, achy *and* cranky. We may not be able to control the rainy weather, but we can be grateful that the grass is getting watered for free.

Norman Vincent Peale, the author of *The Power of Positive Thinking,* writes in the introduction to his book that, "Altogether too many people are defeated by the everyday problems of life. They go struggling, perhaps even whining through their days with a sense of dull resentment at what they consider the "bad breaks" life has given them. In a sense there may be such a thing as "the breaks" in this life, but there is also a spirit and method by which we can control and even determine those breaks. It is a pity that people should let themselves be defeated by the problems, cares and difficulties of human existence, and it is also quite unnecessary,"

Perhaps one of the most profound examples of someone who chose his own attitude in the face of obstacles was Viktor Frankl. In his book, *Man's Search for Meaning,* he explains the experiences as a prisoner in Auschwitz, a Nazi concentration camp. It is through this intolerable suffering from hunger, fear, humiliation and injustice that he comes to recognize the important freedom of being able to choose a positive attitude.

"We who lived in concentration camps can remember the men who walked through the huts comforting others, giving away their last piece of bread. They may have been few in number, but they offer sufficient proof that everything can be taken from a man but one thing: the last of the human freedoms–to choose one's attitude in any given set of circumstances, to choose one's own way."

"Even though conditions such as lack of sleep, insufficient food and various mental stresses may suggest that the inmates were bound to react in certain ways, in the final analysis it becomes clear that the sort of person the prisoner became was the result of an inner decision, and not the result of camp influences alone. Fundamentally, therefore, any man can, even under such circumstances, decide what shall become of him–mentally and spiritually."

Viktor Frankl, and the thousands like him who were victims of concentration camps, had every opportunity of becoming negative, pessimistic and angry. Few would fault them for it. However, he recognized man's ability to transcend his circumstances and grasp a hopeful, positive view. It was a choice.

After his three years in Auschwitz, and other Nazi prisons, Frankl finally gained freedom only to learn that his father, mother, brother and wife had died in camps or were sent to the gas ovens. Except for himself and his sister, his entire family perished in these camps. In spite of that, and perhaps in a large part because of it, he went on to gain a position on the Medical Faculty of the University of Vienna and became a successful psychiatrist. His logotherapy clinics became a helpful resource for those who faced distressing anxiety. His therapy consisted of techniques to assist clients to find meaning and a sense of responsibility in their existence. In his own words, "logotherapy...makes the concept of man into a whole...and focuses its attention upon mankind's groping for a higher meaning in life."

It is no surprise that those who make the choice to be positive are focusing their attention on a "higher meaning in life." By the same token, it comes as no surprise that those who continually wallow in negativity, are following the path that Satan maps for them. It becomes a habit that is difficult to break and only by acknowledging and following the heavenly power of our Father and our Savior, can we begin to see the light through the dark clouds.

Peace through Understanding

Where can we turn for peace and joy? Where can we receive solace from the pains and negativity of the world? These questions can be answered easily in the scriptures. "These things I have spoken unto you, that in me ye might have peace. In the world ye shall have tribulation: but be of good cheer; I have overcome the world," (John 16:33).

Our Heavenly Father prepared a plan to enable us to receive a fullness of joy. Understanding "the great plan of happiness" (Alma 42:8) enables us to be positive about our future, slough off negativity and find peace. Understanding the mercy of our Savior, Jesus Christ, is indeed a path to "good cheer." This plan allows us to be perfected through the Atonement, have eternal family relationships, make choices for ourselves and have an opportunity to live in God's presence and share all that He has. It is no wonder that so many missionaries are sent throughout the world to share this wonderful news. Who would not desire peace instead of despair?

"A testimony of salvation can give us hope and purpose as we wrestle with the challenges of life. We can find reassurance in the knowledge that we are children of God and that we lived in His presence before being born on the earth. We can find meaning in our present life, knowing that our actions during mortality influence our eternal destiny. With this knowledge, we can base important decisions on eternal truths rather than on the changing circumstances of life. We can continually improve our relationships with family members, rejoicing in the promise that our families can be eternal. We can find joy in our testimonies of the Atonement and the Lord's commandments, ordinances, covenants, and doctrines, knowing that 'he who doeth the works of righteousness shall receive his reward, even peace in this world, and eternal life in the world to come'"(D&C 59:23) (LDS.org–Topic Definition–Plan of Salvation).

4

GREEN WITH
ENVY–AND MOLD

Aristotle (in Rhetoric) defined envy (phthonos) as "the pain caused by the good fortune of others", while Kant defined it as "a reluctance to see our own well-being overshadowed by another's because the standard we use to see how well off we are is not the intrinsic worth of our own well-being but how it compares with that of others" (Metaphysics of Morals). Envy can range from coveting others' possessions to having an overwhelming "need" to satisfy our egos with power, beauty, or influence. It is a potent human emotion in that it can transform from jealousy to anger, and from anger to aggression. Envy is the feeling which often precedes acts that run the spectrum of cheating on a test, to cheating on a spouse. "Covetousness, envy, jealousy, and greed always escalate into a vicious spiral, as we seek greater and greater gratification but find less and less contentment" (Brent L. Top, "Thou shall Not Covet," *Ensign*, Dec. 1994, 22).

Green-Eyed Monster

Much of our literature, theater and art reflect the power of envy as if it is an entity in itself. It is referred to as a "green-eyed monster" in a line from Shakespeare's *Othello*. In the play, Iago, a high-ranking soldier is envious of Cassio who was promoted above him. He begins by spreading insulting remarks about Cassio's lack of battle experience. He lies about events, creates rumors about affairs that never happened, manipulates others in order to exact revenge on Othello, and finally commits murders in order to hide his conspiracy. Iago recognizes the potential of envy to canker a soul when he declares, "O! beware, my lord, of jealousy; It is the green-ey'd monster which doth mock The meat it feeds on" (Act III, scene iii).

It is mentioned again in *The Merchant of Venice* when Portia speaks her famous line just as Bassanio begins to open the leaden casket, "How all the other passions fleet to air, As doubtful thoughts, and rash-despair, And shuddering fear, and green-eyed jealousy!" (Act III, scene ii).

To illustrate how one might fall prey to the damaging effects of this "green-eyed monster," consider the following parable: A certain boy with hunger in his eyes journeyed to the refrigerator and openeth the door. He looked for his cheese. He loved the cheese and it was good to the taste. It always satisfied his hunger and gave him peace. He looked in to feast his eyes upon the cheese but his gaze strayed to a colorful jar, instead. It wasn't like anything he had cast his eyes upon before. The container was intriguing and held within it stripes of alternating peanut butter and jelly. The boy had never beheld such a sight as this.

The boy openeth the jar. He ate the contents thereof and found them to be delightful. He spreadeth the peanut butter and jelly on his crackers. He ate. He spreadeth the contents once again on bread, then apples and finally reached his hand forth and dipped his fingers into the jar and licked them. The boy soon neglected the cheese. He went to the refrigerator oft, but chose the peanut butter and jelly instead.

Now the cheese sat in the fridge, alone and dejected. The cheese knew that the catsup and mustard were laughing at him. They were taken from the fridge more often now than he was. Loneliness besought him. Each time the refrigerator door opened, the cheese was hopeful of being chosen, but, lo, the peanut butter and jelly were taken up. And it came to pass that the cheese began to envy the chosen jar. He told the broccoli and the lettuce how the jar had cheated him. He boasted about his flavor to the eggs and the sour cream, reminding them how he enhanced their use. He began to devise ways of shoving the jar off the shelf so it would break. The more envious the cheese became, the greener he turned. He began to stinketh and spread foul smells among the contents of the fridge.

And it came to pass that the day came when the boy made his way to the refrigerator and took out the cheese. He found it to be green. He had loved the cheese and could not find it in himself to destroy it. He cut away the green in order to find the yellow goodness he had once remembered. He tasted of the good part. But behold, the taste was bitter. The envy had rotted its core and the cheese no longer provided nourishment. The boy putteth forth his hand, lifted up the cheese and cast it out. And thus it was that the cheese was destroyed because of its envyings.

Like all parables, the moral is sandwiched somewhere between the meat, cheese, bread and lettuce. How often do we envy others for their popularity or beauty? Perhaps we envy their position or status. Maybe we even envy a person's calling in the church and wonder why we weren't "chosen" instead. Sometimes, like the cheese, we begin to feel doubt about our own abilities or worth when we begin to compare our weaknesses with the obvious strengths of others.

Most of us have had feelings of jealousy or envy at some time. As a Danish proverb suggests, "If envy were a fever, all the world would be ill." We would hardly be human if we had not felt the pangs of covetousness. However, what is most important is what we choose to do or how we choose to act as a result of those feelings. Like the cheese, we could murmur to others about how we have been wronged and pass along some insulting remarks while we are at it. We could put on a show of false bravado to cover our fear of being unpopular, or of underachieving. We could even go as far as to devise a plan for the demise of the offending party, but none of these choices ever brings satisfaction and true happiness.

Envy can become that canker that turns us green and stinky, too. Boasting and spreading gossip and ill will are never attractive attributes. We can become foul with our actions and as a result, be snubbed by the very social circles in which we wanted to be included. But perhaps, even more lamentable is the thought of being cast out of God's presence as a result of the "green-eyed monster." We can allow this feeling to rot us to the core where there was once much goodness. We can allow it to permeate our souls until we are no longer of use, but must be cast aside so as not to cause the decay of others in our presence. As James stated, "For where envying and strife is, there is confusion and every evil work" (James 3:16).

Elder Jeffrey R. Holland of the quorum of the Twelve Apostles, gives some insight into the pervasiveness of envy and jealousy as he explains the parable of the prodigal son. We know that one son squandered his inheritance and was lost to his father, but Elder Holland explains that there were actually *two* sons who were lost. Upon the return of his brother, the elder son becomes angry and will not go in to greet him. "This son is not so much angry that the other brother has come home as he is angry that his parents are so happy about it. Feeling unappreciated and perhaps more than a little self-pity, this dutiful son—and he is wonderfully dutiful—forgets for a moment that he has never had to know filth or despair, fear or self-loathing. He forgets for a moment that every calf on the ranch is already his and so are all the robes in the closet and every ring in the drawer. He forgets for a moment that his faithfulness has been and always will be rewarded.

"Certainly this younger brother had been a prisoner—a prisoner of sin, stupidity, and a pigsty. But the older brother lives in some confinement, too. He has, as yet, been unable to break out of the prison of himself. He is haunted by the green-eyed monster of jealousy. He feels taken for granted by his father and disenfranchised by his brother, when neither is the case. He has fallen victim to a fictional affront. As such he is like Tantalus of Greek mythology—he is up to his chin in water, but he remains thirsty nevertheless. One who has heretofore presumably been very happy with his life and content with his good fortune suddenly feels very unhappy simply because another had had some good fortune as well" (Jeffrey R. Holland, "The Other Prodigal," *Liahona*, Jul 2002, 70).

The older brother in the parable was perhaps unaware of his envy. Had he been able to view his brother as just that–a brother–rather than a rival, he could have rejoiced upon his return. He could have had the opportunity to enjoy their relationship, had he not viewed it as a threat or a competition.

That is the challenge when we recognize this feeling of envy regarding the accom-plishments of others. If we were able to accept them as our brothers and sisters and as children of the same God, we could relish in their successes and realize that it does not diminish our own. The poem, *The Cast*, by Carol Lynn Pearson, beautifully exemplifies this message.

> I lost the starring part in Our Town
> To Linda, a girl not half as good as me,
> Who kept her eyes down
> For the whole tryout, and even stuttered.
>
> When the cast was posted
> And the high school drama coach
> Saw me reading it through my tears,
> He put an arm around me and said,
> "Now, look–things are not always as they
> appear.
> This is not Broadway;
> It's an educational institution.
> We're here for two reasons–to put on a show,
> And, more important, to help people grow.
> Someday you'll see."
>
> So Linda played Emily,

And she didn't even stutter.
And I was Third Woman at the Wedding,
Watching and wondering how he knew
What she could do
If she had the chance.

Since then I have guessed that God,
Being a whole lot smarter
Than my high school drama coach,
Might be offstage sometimes
With an arm around a questioning cast:
"Now, don't try to outguess me.
Sometimes the first shall be last
And the last shall be first,
And I've got my own reasons.
I need some strong ones to star
And some strong ones to stand back.
And I'm going to put out front
Some you might not choose,
But you'll see what they can really do
When they have the chance.
Mortality is an educational institution.
We've got to put on the show,
And, too, we've got to help people grow."

As I walk through the scenes,
Watch the costumes move,
And listen to the lines
Of the powerful, the weak,
The rich, the poor,
I look at the leads with less awe than most,
And at the spear-carriers with more.

Desire vs. Envy

I have observed the tenuous balance that comes with the quest to acquire a material possession or the mission to attain a desired position. I think most of us are motivated by the possibility of getting ahead, of attaining something better or of making our situations more comfortable. The American dream is an attempt to transform hard work into material wealth that can be used for advancement, education or comfort of family members. Even Paul, when speaking to the Corinthians, admonishes them in a positive sense to "covet earnestly the best gifts" (1 Cor.12:31). The difficulty comes when wealth becomes and idol, desire changes to entitlement and ambition turns to greed.

I have long been intrigued by the moral lesson of *The Pearl*, a seemingly simple book written by John Steinbeck. Kino is a pearl diver who provides a meager subsistence for his wife Juana and their son, Coyotito. When a scorpion stings his son, Kino searches for a pearl in order to pay for a doctor to heal him.

The people in Kino's village have a prophesy about a great "Pearl That Might Be," and Kino miraculously emerges from the sea with a pearl as large as a seagull's egg and as "perfect as the moon." The pearl not only becomes a solution to the problem of the doctor, but quickly fills Kino and Juana with hope for their son's future and for the possibility of a life free from oppression. But, although the story reads much like a parable, it is not a fairy tale, and the family does not "live happily ever after." The circumstances that occur after that point and Kino's response to them are more like a tragic novel.

Once the village people behold the pearl and recognize its beauty and size, destructive influences begin to complicate the family's simple life. Powerful and dishonest men connive to take his wealth away. Kino, himself, begins to focus on the sale of the pearl with more determination and ambition, forgetting his initial joy and hope upon its discovery.

Tragedy occurs and Kino and Juana's dreams are violently dashed when Coyotito is killed. Their lives are changed irreparably and the pearl becomes a symbol of evil and destruction. The book concludes with Kino casting the pearl back into the sea, a renunciation of all that the pearl represents.

Upon my initial reading of the book, I quickly became an advocate for Kino. He worked hard. He was met with good fortune for his efforts. His hope for a secure future for his wife and son were commendable. But, the shift in his focus from his family's health and security to his acquisition of material wealth and status caused my opinion to change, and the subtlety with which this occurred was as interesting as the shift itself.

Kino had every right to negotiate the sell of the pearl for its real monetary value. He sought to create a future for himself. His struggle to resist those who would control and exploit him was an honest attempt. I found those admirable qualities. But slowly, Kino began to devote more time and energy toward the pearl's protection, and greed started to seep into the cracks of his character like trickling water onto dry sand. Juana, his wife, was not certain if his intentions were genuine, but Kino seemed to be able to justify his actions.

This is this same subtlety with which Satan is able to cause our priorities to change. It is not swift and obvious. It is with quiet and conniving skill that this great deceiver is able to change our idea of financial security to sacrificing our values for more material gain. It is why Paul the Apostle cautioned Timothy that "the love of money is the root of all evil: which while some coveted after, they have erred from the faith, and pierced themselves through with many sorrows" (1 Timothy 6:10).

We are all vulnerable to the spirit of covetousness. Careful balance is required to keep us from the slippery slope of acquisition of material goods to an all-consuming focus to acquire more. There is danger in forgetting eternal objectives when our "hearts are set so much upon the things of this world..." (D&C 121:35).

When I was a young girl, I enjoyed paper dolls. When the McCall's Magazine would come in the mail, I would eagerly turn the pages until I found Betsy. Betsy McCall had new clothes every month and for every occasion. I would carefully cut out Betsy, have her try on her new dresses, then place them in the shoe box with the others I had collected. Although Betsy's wardrobe seemed to be more than adequate, I felt she required a spacious bedroom in which to store her clothing. I thumbed through the Sears Catalogue until I found the bedroom furniture and bedspread that I was certain she would love. I cut it out and arranged it on the living room floor. It was lovely. But why stop with just a bedroom? Soon I had cut out curtains, sofas, dining room tables, and bathroom fixtures. These were all stored in the shoe box and taken out regularly to arrange for Betsy. When the next seasonal catalogue would come in the mail, Betsy's furniture was easily replaced with new and improved pieces.

I still enjoy looking at catalogues and magazines that seem to come in the mail with much more frequency. On occasion, I cut out the pictures of the furniture arrangements and decorating ideas and save them for my next "project." I also frequent home shows to view the latest designs, and watch HGTV with more than enthusiasm.

A few years ago after attending one such parade of homes, I observed the new kitchens being presented and one thing became painfully apparent; mine was out of date. These new kitchens had cabinets made of alder wood, appliances made of stainless steel, counter-tops made of granite and light fixtures that were not only efficient, but stylish. My refrigerator was an almond color, and according to the salesman at the appliance store, "They don't even make them in that color anymore." My counter-tops were laminate that looked pretty good twenty years ago when they were installed. The stools at the counter didn't match and one had been glued back together a few times. My pink and green floral wallpaper was still happily intact, but was probably better suited for a bathroom built in the fifties. Amazingly, I hadn't even been aware of those deficiencies until I compared my kitchen to the new and improved ones that "everyone else" had!

But, of course, "everyone else" does not have these material things. In fact, not everyone has a kitchen with tables and chairs and hot water and food in the fridge. It's important to keep our desires in perspective and recognize the blessings instead of staring into the magnifying glass to observe all that we don't have. It is too easy to begin estimating our material assets and subtracting everything that is wrong while neglecting to add all that we have and all that is right.

President Hinckley said, "... none of us ever has enough-at least that is what we think. No matter our financial circumstances, we want to improve them. This, too, is good if it is not carried to an extreme. I am satisfied that the Father of us all does not wish His children to walk in poverty. He wants them to have comforts and some of the good things of the earth.... He would have His children properly fed and clothed and sheltered, enjoying the comforts that come of the earth, but not to excess. It is when greed takes over, when we covet that which others have, that our affliction begins. And it can be a very sore and painful affliction ("Thou Shalt Not Covet," *Ensign*, March 1990, 2).

The Greek philosopher, Epicurus, gave us wise counsel when he cautioned, "Do not spoil what you have by desiring what you have not; remember that what you now have was once among the things you only hoped for."

The Disguises of Envy

The envy that sometimes follows admiration of material possessions is much like the envy that can result when contrasting our perceived personal deficiencies with others' obvious assets. Rather than admiring a person's strengths, talents or beauty, we sometimes allow ourselves to be irritated by them. Rather than complimenting them, we tend to find fault with them and rather than supporting them, we tend to sabotage them.

We often don't recognize the feeling of envy in ourselves because it is disguised as criticism or fault finding. Think of the time when someone told you about a wonderful play they attended or an exciting trip they took. Were you quick to show interest, or did you skillfully squelch their enthusiasm by diminishing their activity? When someone you know achieved success, did you compliment them or begrudge them?

We do live in a society that compares people according to their beauty or intelligence or athletic ability. There are often accolades and awards presented to those who perform in the public spotlight. A testament to that is the publication of the numerous magazines and tabloids touting the rise to fame of the most recent celebrity. And I can't even count the number of television broadcasts that glorify the movie, shoes, hair, smile, clothing, car, vacations or boyfriends of the latest star. We look forward to the next luscious morsel of news and eat it up like a kid who has anxiously waited all day for the ice cream truck to drive down his street.

But as popular as it is to publish and produce the celebrity good news of the day, it is just as popular, if not more so, to reveal stories about a celebrity's financial problem, marital problem, legal problem or health problem. The hunger for this type of news may be a disguise of envy as well. We could have admired a person for his talents or accomplishments and then felt genuine sorrow when he or she fell upon difficulties. But more often than not, we feel envious of that person and are now secretly happy that he is suffering. It somehow makes us feel better about ourselves and legitimizes our envy.

Jefferey R. Holland explains, "We see allurements of one kind or another that tell us what we have is not enough. Someone or something is forever telling us we need to be wealthier, more handsome, more applauded or more admired than we see ourselves as being. We are told we haven't collected enough possessions or gone to enough fun places. We are bombarded with the message that on the word's scale of things we have been weighed in the balance and found wanting. Some days it is as if we have been locked in a cubicle of a great and spacious building where the only thing on TV is a never-ending soap opera entitled *Vain Imaginations*" ("The Other Prodigal," *Liahona*, Jul 2002, 69-72).

As a teacher and counselor in middle school and high school, I had the dubious opportunity to observe the behaviors that were influenced by envy. In fact, there was a veritable workshop of examples! It seemed difficult for some students to celebrate another's happiness or good fortune, often because they felt it somehow diminished their own self importance. This was displayed in behaviors such as gossiping, name-calling, eye rolling, bullying and other practices. Seldom did the student recognize or admit the behaviors may be a result of their feeling of envy which caused an "us against them" attitude.

It can be difficult to avoid the feeling of envy in every situation. But if envy is allowed to grow and is nurtured by continual resentment, it can wreak havoc on our behavior and our spirits.

Seven Deadly Sins

Envy has been classified as one of the seven deadly sins by spiritual writers and theologians of early Christian history. These seven sins were not considered so grievous because of their singular severity, but more because they were inevitable sources of greater transgressions that could be fatal to spiritual progress. By examining some Biblical examples, one can easily observe the escalation of envy as it quickly moves from a feeling to a violent act.

Daniel and certain Hebrews had been trained in the court of Nebuchadnezzar, but had maintained his faithfulness to God. Because of this, he was in God's favor and had received great knowledge and wisdom. Daniel proved himself to be such a valuable asset to the king, that when Darius became the new King of Persia, he appointed Daniel as first of his presidents to rule over the princes of the kingdom. "Then this Daniel was preferred above the presidents and princes. Because an excellent spirit was in him; and the king thought to set him over the whole realm" (Daniel 6:3).

This act caused much jealousy among the other presidents and princes. They, no doubt, believed they should have been the ones to receive this great favor from the king, and because Daniel was chosen instead, they immediately began to think of ways to discredit him.

"Then the presidents and princes sought to find occasion against Daniel concerning the kingdom..." (Daniel 6:4).

Finally, the presidents, governors, princes and counselors consulted together and devised a royal statute that would trap Daniel by making it illegal for him or anyone else to "ask a petition of God or man for thirty days," save it be the king. They convinced Darius to sign the document thereby making it a mandatory law for all his subjects to worship only him during that time; the consequences of breaking the law would result in being cast into a den of lions (Daniel 6:7).

Daniel, in spite of the decree, made no attempt to hide his prayers and thanks before his God. He was placed in the den of lions as a result, but God sent his angel and shut the lions' mouths; he was delivered from their power. King Darius was overjoyed and gave the order to have the men who had falsely accused Daniel to suffer his same judgment. He further decreed that everyone in his kingdom would worship the God of Daniel (Daniel 6:10-27).

It is interesting to note that Daniel received his appointment from the king without seeking it out or campaigning for it. He also had not received the honor by adjusting his beliefs to fit the occasion, or by contriving to slander or degrade others who were in his path on the ladder of success. And it is also important to recognize that even the other presidents, "could find none occasion nor fault; forasmuch as he was faithful, neither was there any error or fault found in him" (Daniel 6:4). They simply envied Daniel because he had received such good fortune. Despite the fact that they themselves were in positions of leadership over the kingdom and had chains of gold about their necks, they could not feel contentment in their hearts.

Let us consider that last statement: *They* could not feel contentment in *their* hearts. Did each prince and president have envy in his own heart? Did each one individually contrive to expel Daniel? Could the plan have been carried out without group consent?

Envy is a thought or a feeling. But those thoughts can easily be allowed to invade like a cancer cell that metastasizes and grows more powerful as tentacles sprout from its origin. Soon Lucifer, the father of all lies, allows us to believe the subtle but evil whisperings of men, until we become convinced that we are justified in acting upon our thoughts. We are counseled, "Be not thou envious against evil men, neither desire to be with them. For their heart studieth destruction, and their lips talk of mischief" (Proverbs 24:1-2).

In Genesis, we are introduced to the brothers of Joseph who also "talk of mischief." The eleventh son of Jacob, "the son of his old age," Joseph was loved and favored of his father. As a symbol of that love, Jacob made Joseph a coat of many colors. (Gen. 37: 3) This caused much jealousy among Joseph's brothers and they "could not speak peaceably unto him" (Gen. 37: 4).

When Joseph told them of his dreams that indicated he would rule over them, "they hated him all the more for his dreams, and for his words" (Gen. 37:8). Rather than rejoicing with their younger brother that he may have this honor bestowed upon him, "his brethren envied him" (Gen. 37: 11).

When Joseph was seventeen, his father sent him to inquire after his brothers who were pasturing flocks of sheep. He approached his brothers and "even before he came near unto them, they conspired against him to slay him" (Gen. 37:18). Ruben, however, convinced the others to throw him into a pit instead. Eventually, Joseph was lifted out of the pit and sold to Ishmaelites for twenty pieces of silver and was taken to Egypt.

In Egypt, Joseph was elevated to a position of authority and thus had the opportunity to rescue his family from the famine in Canaan. However, the brothers had anguished for many years over their actions as they said one to another, "We are verily guilty concerning our brother, in that we saw the anguish of his soul, when he besought us, and we would not hear; therefore is this distress come upon us" (Gen. 42: 21).

The stories of Daniel and Joseph illustrate the danger of allowing the feeling of envy to fester until we find ourselves guilty of other, more serious sins. We do ourselves an injustice by allowing envy to alienate us from the Lord and our fellowmen. What satisfaction could come into our lives if we would allow ourselves to rejoice in the blessings of others instead?

In contrast to the brothers of Joseph, one need only recognize the devotion of the brother of Joseph Smith. Hyrum accepted the calling that Joseph had received from the Lord. He supported him rather than envied him. He served under the direction of his younger brother in duties ranging from clearing weeds to carrying the translated manuscripts to the typesetter. Hyrum strengthened his brother rather than criticized him.

President Heber J. Grant said of Hyrum Smith: "There is no better example of an older brother's love than that exhibited in the life of Hyrum Smith for the Prophet Joseph Smith. ...They were as united and as affectionate and as loving as mortal men could be. ...There never was one particle of ...jealousy ...in the heart of Hyrum Smith. No mortal man could have been more loyal, more true, more faithful in life or in death than was Hyrum Smith to the Prophet of the living God" ("Hyrum Smith and His Distinguished Posterity," *Improvement Era*, Aug.1918, 854-55).

The choice that Hyrum made, to be supportive of his brother rather than envious of his calling and commission, increases our regard for him. It increases our esteem rather than diminishing it. It makes him appear nobler and more courageous.

Maintaining the perspective required to support a brother rather than envy and degrade him, requires us to love and respect ourselves. "And let every man esteem his brother as himself, and practice virtue and holiness before me. And again I say unto you. Let every man esteem his brother as himself" (D&C:38:24-25). Perhaps that is what was lacking in the Hebrews and the brothers of Joseph.

Daniel, Joseph of Egypt and Joseph Smith all suffered the criticism and envy of their fellow men. Joseph Smith found comfort and support from his brother, Hyrum. However, as we study the lives of each of these men, we come to realize that as targets of envy, they, too, could have become hardened. They could have succumbed to the criticism. They could have exacted revenge and become as wicked as those who targeted them. Instead, each continued on with his life mission and showed love to those who spitefully found fault with them. It is a great lesson for each of us.

Although we may never encounter the torture or the severity of the forces of jealousy and envy that Daniel and the Josephs suffered, we all need to be reminded to guard ourselves from those who may wish to take us down with their envy.

Og Mandino reminds us of "a better way to live." "Remember that envy, like the worm, is always attracted to the fairest apple. You cannot make progress in your life as a hermit, and so you must make contact with the world and its parade of misfortunes and critics, yet you need never allow either to rain on your parade. Turn away from the envious" (Og Mandino, *A Better Way to Live*, 115).

5

THIS GRUDGE IS GETTING HEAVY

A classic story by Guy de Maupassant tells the tale of Maitre Hauchecome, a peasant from the country who had come to Goderville for market day. As he approached the public square, he noticed a piece of string upon the ground. Being the economical man he was, he picked it up from the ground thinking it may be useful at some later time. As he wound the string, he noticed Maitre Malandain, the harness maker, on the threshold of his door, looking at him. They had previous business together concerning a halter, and they were currently "on bad terms, both being good haters." Maitre Hauchecome felt embarrassed having his enemy, Malandain see him pick up string from the dirt, so he quickly concealed the string under his blouse and then in the pocket of his trousers.

Later in the day, as the crowds in the square began to thin, some of the people, including Hauchecome, gathered at the local tavern for food and drink and chatter. Suddenly, the drum beat of the public crier was heard. He announced to the inhabitants of the town that a black leather pocketbook had been lost and the finder was requested to return it to the mayor's office for a reward. People began to talk of the event when shortly thereafter, an officer came to the tavern asking for Maitre

Hauchecome to come with him. It seemed that the harness maker had told the mayor that he had seen Hauchecome earlier that day as he picked up something out of the dirt and hid it suspiciously on his person. Hauchecome was offended and furious. He showed the mayor the piece of string and repeated his innocence. It was of little use, for no one believed him.

On his way home, Hauchcome repeated the story to three neighbors. He went out of his way before going home in order to tell a few more. He was ill all night.

The next day, a hired man who had found the wallet returned it to its owner. He said he had found the object on the road, but not knowing how to read, had carried it to his employer first. When the news spread to Hauchecome, he immediately went the circuit and began to recount his innocence to anyone who would listen. He told people coming out of church; he told complete strangers. But, there was the nagging thought that people still didn't believe him and considered him to be an accomplice. "He was stricken to the heart by the injustice of the suspicion."

He became consumed in his effort to defend himself. The more he did, the more suspicion the townspeople had. "His mind, touched to the depth, began to weaken." He finally died, and in the delirium of his death he kept claiming his innocence, reiterating: "A piece of string, a piece of string–look-here it is, M'sieu the Mayor " (www.classicshorts. com/string).

By their very nature, grudges are one of the most detrimental obstacles in the path of our personal happiness. As with Hauchecome, we cannot always change the circumstances that beset us or the accusations that come against us. We can, however, choose how we will respond to them. And, like the peasant in the story, we will find no peace of mind in nurturing a grudge.

Grudges Cause Personal Harm

There was a group of men on a backpacking trip. Two of the men were very good friends in spite of the fact they often played mischievous but harmless pranks on each other. One of the friends, "Bill," managed to sneak some stones into "Jim's" backpack each time the group stopped for water or rest. Jim commented to the others how heavy his pack felt and mentioned more than once that he must be out of shape. Each time he would pull his arms through the pack and strap it to his waist again, he would shake his head at the punishment he was inflicting upon himself by carrying around the heavy backpack.

Finally, Bill confessed the prank and helped Jim throw away the rocks in his pack. Each had a good laugh, and Jim was delighted to find how light his burden was after the heavy stones had been discarded.

Carrying grudges is much like picking up a pack full of rocks and strapping it to our back. It weighs us down. It becomes a burden. It causes fatigue and pain and can even injure us if we continue to punish ourselves by leaving it in place.

Grudges seldom hurt the person who wronged us. Instead, we hurt ourselves by carrying them around. If we look at it in terms of physical rocks causing physical injury, it's easier to see the danger. When our pain is an emotional burden, it is difficult to recognize the harm being caused. We minimize and underestimate the susceptibility to high blood pressure, fatigue, or headaches. We take pain relievers instead of relieving ourselves of the weight of the grudge.

"Grudges are actually a major source of chronic stress to you, and chronic stress has been linked to illnesses including heart disease, cancer, depression, autoimmune diseases and reproductive problems, along with more minor maladies like stomach upset, back pain, headaches and fatigue. So not surprisingly, when you let go of a grudge, you can expect to feel like a weight has been lifted off of your shoulders, both figuratively and literally" (www. sedona.com).

Why do we refuse to forget every insult we have ever received or every negative look that was sent our way? Why do we carry grudges for weeks, months or years? If we actually realized the mental and physical drain of all-consuming grudges, we would question why we persist in carrying them.

Perhaps the need to harbor a grudge has to do with our normal desire to be noticed. We can evoke sympathy from our friends and family members by letting them in on the injustices we have suffered. They will likely respond with the needed attention—at least for the first few times.

There is a temporary sense of satisfaction when we can toss out a grudge in conversation and receive sympathy from our listeners. They may reassure us that we didn't deserve the injustice, that we were wronged. They may console us and comfort us or compliment us for our strength in carrying such a burden. We may feel justified in our grudge and resolve to carry it even longer. But the satisfaction is fleeting when we recognize that the listeners stop listening and the comforters stop comforting and we lose the desired attention. In reality, even the most compassionate listener gets tired of the "pack of rocks" you are carrying and is wondering why you don't drop it!

It could also be that keeping a grudge gives us the illusion of having control and therefore being resistant to being hurt. Actually, just the opposite is true. Maybe we keep a grudge brewing because we don't think the other person should be let off the hook. Maybe it's just easier to blame someone else than to admit any personal responsibility.

Perhaps we hold on to a grudge because of our pride. We think of it as a noble cause and foresee the day of our triumph when we will be able to get even or take our revenge. We are the winner if we do not "back down." In order to do this, we need to dwell on the events that caused us the pain. We need to replay the situations over and over in our minds. We need to be consumed with the injustice. We need to nurture our resentment, tend our wounds and plant vengeance so it can take root.

When we examine our motives in this light, we begin to see more clearly what we are doing to ourselves. There is no reward in resurrecting painful events. There is no solace in resentment and bitterness. There is no payback for wallowing in self-pity. We are the ones who pay the price. We are the person being harmed.

A vivid example from our American history illustrates the detrimental effect on the life of a person who harbors a grudge. The name, Benedict Arnold, is most commonly associated with the terms "traitor" or "treason." However, the man, Benedict Arnold, is considered by many historians to have been one of the most brilliant and accomplished leaders in the Continental Army. Without his contributions in the capture of Fort Ticonderoga, the Battle of Saratoga and other successful campaigns, the American Revolution may have had a different outcome.

In spite of Arnold's military successes, he was passed over for promotion in favor of less experienced officers. "This act by the Continental Congress incensed Arnold, who felt his efforts on behalf of the revolution were not being recognized. Frustrated, bitter, disaffected by the assaults on his honor and strongly opposed to the new American alliance with France, Arnold changed sides" (http:www.benedictarnold.org).

He devised a scheme to obtain command of West Point, then surrender it to the British. Because of his service to the British, he was given a commission as a Brigadier General in their army. Although he had the title, the loyalists did not embrace and support the man. With little to do, he sailed with his wife to England.

"Though he makes every attempt to place himself in friendship with prominent Tories, including King George, he is for the most part ignored. In 1785, frustrated by the army's unwillingness to grant him any further command, he sails to Canada and embarks on a business career, which fares no better. He returns to England in 1791, spends his final years as a bitter, dejected man, whose dreams of fortune and fame die with him in 1801. He is sixty" (Jeff Shaara, *The Glorious Cause*, 677).

Although Arnold could have been recognized in our history as a hero, his bitterness created a very different and unfortunate end to his story. His constant grudge against those who failed to recognize his efforts, caused him personal strife and stripped away his opportunity for a satisfying future. While he may have felt he was "getting even" with those who insulted him, he was the one who suffered in the end.

Several years ago, a family member of mine was dismissed from his employment by a board of directors with an "agenda." There was nothing in his conduct or written in his file that would have warranted the act. It was simply a decision made by persons who considered it a needed change. The negative media coverage and seemingly lack of support he received angered me. I was hurt because someone had hurt him. I conjured up bitter comments and replayed them in my mind. At one point, I decided I would move out of the community and to another state so that I wouldn't have to associate with people such as these. I allowed the situation to create a considerable amount of emotional turmoil and physical stress.

Another family member talked with me about the situation. They had been hurt, too. But they were wise enough to help me realize that hanging on to my grudge would only be hurtful to me. It would not bother the majority of the community if I moved from it. On the other hand, I would be leaving the majority of my family, my friends, my job and my home! This was only one bad circumstance. Life works that way sometimes. Leaving everything that I loved in order to "show them," would be counterproductive and more harmful to me than the circumstance itself. Thankfully, I was able to give up the revenge plot and the U-Haul idea. I stayed in the same community and found joy in the place and the people.

President Gordon B. Hinckley said, "I submit that it takes neither strength nor intelligence to brood in anger over wrongs suffered, to go through life with a spirit of vindictiveness, to dissipate one's abilities in planning retribution. There is no peace in the nursing of a grudge. There is no happiness in living for the day when you can 'get even.'

"Paul speaks of the 'weak and beggarly elements' of our lives (Gal. 4:9). Is there anything more weak or beggarly than the disposition to wear out one's life in an unending round of bitter thoughts and scheming gestures toward those who may have affronted us?" ("'Of You It Is Required to Forgive'" *Ensign*, Nov. 1980, 61).

Grudges Harm Our Relationships

I've heard the saying many times: "Don't make a mountain out of a molehill." And yet, I have seen many examples of families and friends who have been torn apart by tiny molehills of hurt that have erupted into volcanic mountains of grudges. There are brothers and sisters who haven't spoken to their siblings in years. There are adult children who haven't been home to see their parents, not because of distance or finances, but because of strained relationships. Families fight over the estate of their elderly parents who have passed away. Spouses nurture grudges and bring up old hurts. Friends, neighbors and business associates refuse to settle their differences.

Sometimes we hold on to a grudge while waiting for the offending party to apologize first. Sometimes we hang on to grudges while we wait for the other person to change. Some tenaciously keep a grip on injustices received from the government, life, or God, waiting for them *all* to change. What a waste of valuable time! We could be spending the time strengthening our own weaknesses or initiating positive changes rather than focusing our time and energy on waiting for others to conform.

One mother found that her relationship with her daughter was salvaged when a friend gave her some stinging but helpful advice about holding grudges. She and her family had been active in the Church, had taught their family the Gospel and tried their best to live it. They were disappointed, however, when their daughter became engaged to a nonmember. As the mother talked to her friend, she told her that she was angry and felt betrayed by her daughter and didn't want to give her a wedding or even see her. She received this reply:

"'What kind of a mother are you that you only love her when she does what you want her to do. That is selfish, self centered, qualified love.

It's easy to love our children when they are good; but when they make mistakes, they need our love even more. We should love and care for them no matter what they do. It doesn't mean we condone or approve of the errors, but we help, not condemn; love, not hate; forgive, not judge. We build them up rather than tear them down; we lead them, not desert them. We love when they are the most unlovable, and if you can't or won't do that, you are a poor mother.'

"With tears streaming down her face, the mother asked her friend how she could ever thank her. The friend answered, 'Do it for someone else when the need arises. Someone did it for me, and I will be eternally grateful" (Jack H Goaslind, "Reach Out to Our Father's Children," *Ensign*, May 1981, 59).

In a middle school group counseling activity, I asked students to take three minutes to respond to situations that caused them stress. I provided pencils and a stack of small note cards for each student. They were to write one response on each card, toss it into the middle of the table, and continue until they had either exhausted their stressors or until time was up. When the timer started, there was feverish writing and I was surprised by the stack of cards that were quickly multiplying on the table. When the cards were collected and read aloud, the responses included such things as "bad grades" or "bullies," but the vast majority of the students wrote, "my sister, my father, my brother, my mother, my friends."

It became apparent as we continued to discuss these important, but strained relationships, that many were suffering as a result of hurtful words or actions. Whether the experiences were real or perceived, recent or years in the past, the students were swallowed up in their hurt or bitterness or sense of injustice. These feelings that could have been eliminated quickly, were growing, festering and becoming more powerful and overwhelming. They were now grudges fueled by anger and resentment.

As the group sessions continued, the students learned strategies for strengthening those relationships and brainstormed solutions that they could try. Most often, they recognized their part in the growing chasm of the relationship. In most cases, there was reconciliation or at least a state of peaceful understanding. The process was not always easy or swift. "A brother offended is harder to be won than a strong city and their bars are like castles" (Prov. 18:19). All agreed, however, that it was worth it.

Close relationships allow us to learn cooperation, respect and compromise. We can share experiences, receive support, identify our role in the human family and feel security and love. Positive relationships are essential to our emotional well-being. Psychologists have suggested that, "all humans have a motivational drive to form and maintain caring interpersonal relationships. According to this view, people need both stable relationships and satisfying interactions with the people in those relationships. If either of these two ingredients is missing, people will begin to feel anxious, lonely, depressed, and unhappy" (Baumeister, R. F., & Leary, M. R. (1995) "The Need to Belong: Desire for Interpersonal Attachments as a Fundamental Human Motivation" *Psychological Bulletin, 117,* 497-529). Yet, there are those who spend more time and energy at "getting their way" or "being right" than they do at forgiving and working at a valued relationship. I don't know of anyone who, at the end of his life, finds more satisfaction from winning an argument, than from healing a scarred relationship.

I had an experience that helped me realize how grudges keep us from enjoying some of our most important relationships. I think it is still so vivid in my memory because of the emotional impact it had on me. I was traveling by myself after visiting relatives in Belgium. I took my assigned seat on the plane in anticipation of the long, fourteen-hour journey across the ocean. I had a good book and my crocheting project, so I settled in for a quiet time of solitude. I'm not wild about visiting with the strangers sitting next to me, so I opened my book and quickly stuck my nose in it to signal my lack of interest.

Although my head was down and my attention was diverted, I couldn't ignore the loud conversation going on over my head and beside me. A woman was very upset with her seat assignment because she was sitting across the plane from her husband and children. I finally caught on that I was the one sitting next to her husband. I excused myself for overhearing their conversation, and volunteered to move across the plane. I figured I could ignore those passengers just as well on that side. I settled in once again, giving a quick smile to the young man next to me, and found my place in the book. My plan was going well.

An hour passed and I transferred the book to my bag and pulled out my crocheting. I think that's what sparked the interest in the young man on my left. Either he was very bored or just curious about what I was making, but the questions and conversation began. He was adorable and about the age of my oldest son, so I had a hard time snubbing his questions.

It seems that in starting a conversation, the common questions asked are, "Where are you from?" and "What do you do?" I suppose it helps us relate our situation to theirs in an attempt to find common ground and expand the conversation. So I was not surprised when he asked the daunting question, "What do you do?" And, because I have had similar experiences before, I wasn't too surprised at what transpired from that point.

When I told him I was a counselor, the conversation became more involved and soon became the longest counseling session I have ever encountered! He told me about his family situation and how his relationship with his mother was less than satisfying. He had obviously been hurt and as a result held on to the grudge. He had little conversation with her and had seldom been home, even for holidays. As he continued, he said several times, "But I don't care." "But it doesn't matter to me."

Obviously, it *did* matter. He had just spent the last hour and a half talking about it! The funny thing was, I didn't mind. As a counselor, I was learning from him how detrimental it was to hold a grudge and I could see his anguish because of it. As a mother, I could sense the loss I would feel if my children harbored those feelings against me. As we continued to talk, he started to accept the possibility that his mother may never change, but there was much he could do to change his feelings toward her. We discussed strategies for establishing a relationship with certain boundaries. We talked of how he could heal even if the relationship did not.

It broke my heart to see the misery that this young man was going through. It helped me realize that much of our misery is caused by our unwillingness to let go of it. A grudge can harm the one who carries it, but it also alienates the very people who could bring us the most joy, comfort, and support. The experience was a fresh reminder for me to strengthen my relationships with my own family. I believe that both of us benefited that day from our "chance" meeting.

The actions or words of others have great potential for offending us. How we respond to these offenses is often the determining factor between continuing a friendship, or creating an enemy. I love the example in the Book of Mormon of Pahoran and his encounter with the strong and bitter words of Captain Moroni.

Moroni was grieved concerning the wickedness of his people and how many were being slaughtered by the hands of the Lamanites. He was angry with the Chief Judge, Pahoran, because of the seeming neglect by the government to supply his armies. He wrote to the governor and to those who were managing the affairs of the war. He told them of the sufferings of his armies from "hunger and thirst, and fatigue, and all manner of afflictions of every kind" (Alma 60:3).

His begrudgement is apparent as he writes: "Ye have neglected them insomuch that the blood of thousands shall come upon your heads for vengeance; yea, for known unto God were all their cries, and all their sufferings... Behold, could ye suppose that ye could sit upon your thrones and because of the exceeding goodness of God ye could do nothing and he would deliver you? Behold, if ye have supposed this ye have supposed in vain. I fear exceedingly that the judgments of God will come upon this people, because of their exceeding slothfulness, yea, even the slothfulness of our government and their exceedingly great neglect...(Alma 60:10,11,14).

Unbeknownst to Moroni, Pahoran was also grieved because of the suffering of Moroni's armies. Although he was willing to supply the army with food and men, rebellion and insurrection had arisen in Zerahemla and provisions and men were being withheld. The rebels had appointed a king for themselves and joined an alliance with the Lamanites. Pahoran had been driven out of the city and was in the land of Gideon attempting to gather an army against his perpetrators.

Few people eagerly accept criticism, disapproval and condemnation, even when it is justified. But to remain calm upon being accused of a wrong for which you were *not* responsible, is indeed a mark of strength and Christian character. Pahoran reveals that character when he replies, "And now, in your epistle you have censured me, but it mattereth not; I am not angry, but do rejoice in the greatness of your heart. I, Pahoran, do not seek for power, save only to retain my judgment seat that I may preserve the rights and the liberty of my people"... (Alma 61:9). He continues to write concerning the strategies they both can take to win the war for the liberty of their people, and he closes his letter to his "beloved brother, Moroni" (Alma 61:21).

Most of us have been the object of criticism or condemnation at some point in our lives. Following the example of Pahoran would allow us to be free from the heavy burden of holding a grudge against our accuser or of sacrificing a treasured friendship.

Grudges May Harm Our Salvation

Many of us know of individuals or families that have chosen to stop attending church or participate in church activities because they were offended by a snub or an insulting remark. While the Gospel is perfect, the Church is made up of imperfect people with human frailties attempting the ongoing process of working toward perfection. With that in mind, it is not unlikely that something could be unintentionally said or done that could offend us. While these unfortunate experiences occur, it is our choice as to how we will respond.

Elder David A. Bednar explains, "One of the greatest indicators of our own spiritual maturity is revealed in how we respond to the weaknesses, the inexperience, and the potentially offensive actions of others. A thing, an event, or an expression may be offensive, but you and I can choose not to be offended…To be offended is a *choice* we make; it is not a *condition* inflicted or imposed upon us by someone or something else" ("And Nothing Shall Offend Them," *Liahona*, Nov 2006, 89-92).

In most instances, the offended party has held onto the grudge for personal reasons and forgotten that they have removed themselves from the blessings of the Gospel and opportunity for spiritual growth. Elder Bednar tells of visiting individuals who have done just that. His thought-provoking statements to them are cause for reflection.

"'Let me make sure I understand what has happened to you. Because someone at church offended you, you have not been blessed by the ordinance of the sacrament. You have withdrawn yourself from the constant companionship of the Holy Ghost. Because someone at church offended you, you have cut yourself off from priesthood ordinances and the holy temple. You have discontinued your opportunity to serve others and to learn and grow. And you are leaving barriers that will impede the spiritual progress of your children, your children's children, and the generations that will follow'" ("And Nothing Shall Offend Them," *Liahona*, Nov. 2006, 89-92).

We seldom consider the everlasting effects of a grudge. Recognizing the spiritual harm to ourselves and the potential damage to generations helps us put our choices into perspective.

Choosing not to take offense allows us to rise to a more spiritual plane. Most everyone has been hurt at some time by the words or actions of another person. The decision to let go of resentment and bitterness can greatly reduce the powerful effect these feelings might otherwise have on us. It doesn't minimize or justify the wrong, but it can allow us to focus on more positive aspects of our lives.

The Saints of the early Church were persecuted on numerous occasions. These situations could have caused them to harbor hatred and hostility, but many are the examples of bearing these abuses with meekness rather than revenge.

One of those examples is in the character of Bishop Edward Partridge. "Following the commandment of the Lord, Bishop Partridge purchased hundreds of acres of land in Jackson County, Missouri for the many Saints who were emigrating from Ohio and elsewhere. Local citizens warned Church members that they were displeased with the arrival of so many Latter-day Saints, who, they feared, would soon overwhelm them at the voting polls. The Saints were primarily from the northern states and generally were against black slavery, which was then legal in the state of Missouri. The Saints' belief in the Book of Mormon as scripture, their claim that Jackson County was ultimately to be their Zion, and their assertion that they were led by a prophet were very unsettling. Too, the charge that they had contact with the Indians aroused the suspicions of the local citizens.

"A circular, sometimes referred to as the secret constitution, was passed around by the opposition to obtain the signatures of those willing to eliminate the "Mormon scourge." These feelings of animosity culminated on 20 July 1833 when a mob, numbering some 400 men, met at the courthouse in Independence to coordinate their efforts. Written demands were placed before the leaders of the Church calling upon the Saints to leave Jackson County; to cease printing their newspaper, and not to allow any additional Church members to come into Jackson County. When the mob found that the Church's leaders would not agree to these illegal requirements, they attacked the newspaper office, stole the printing press and demolished the building.

"The mob next seized Bishop Edward Partridge and Charles Allen. They were taken to the public square in Independence and commanded to renounce the Book of Mormon and leave the county. Bishop Partridge said, ""I told them that the Saints had suffered persecution in all ages of the world; that I had done nothing which ought to offend anyone; that if they abused me, they would abuse an innocent person; that I was willing to suffer for the sake of Christ; but, to leave the country, I was not then willing to consent to it.'

"With this refusal, the men were stripped of their outer clothing and their bodies were covered with tar and feathers. Bishop Partridge observed, 'I bore my abuse with so much resignation and meekness, that it appeared to astound the multitude, who permitted me to retire in silence, many looking very solemn, their sympathies having been touched as I thought; and as to myself, I was so filled with the Spirit and love of God, that I had no hatred towards my persecutors or anyone else'" (*Our Heritage: A Brief History of The Church of Jesus Christ of Latter-day Saints,* 37).

This ability to forgive the persons committing the action without justifying the action itself, allowed Bishop Partridge and the others to continue on with their important work rather than to spend time planning retribution. It did not mean that they denied the other person's responsibility for their act, but it did allow them to loose the ties of resentment that would bind them.

While it may seem difficult, even impossible, we can learn from the example of those who have endured devastating afflictions with courage, faith and forgiveness. Another such example is the Amish community in the hills of Pennsylvania. On October 2, 2006, a 32-year-old milk truck driver stormed into a one-room schoolhouse in the Amish community of Nickel Mines, took hostages and eventually shot and killed five girls between the ages of six and thirteen before killing himself. The news was shocking and was instantly reported on television broadcasts and printed in newspapers.

It was difficult to comprehend the motive for such violence. Just as astounding, however, was the response of the Amish toward the family of the milkman. On the day of the shooting, a grandfather of one of the murdered Amish girls was heard warning some young relatives not to hate the killer, saying, 'We must not think evil of this man.' A member of the community living near the Amish explained, 'I don't think there's anybody here that wants to do anything but forgive and not only reach out to those who have suffered a loss in that way but to reach out to the family of the man who committed these acts'" (www.cnn.com/2006/amish.shootings).

Although grieving themselves, the Amish people reached out to the milkman's suffering family by visiting and comforting them. One Amish man held the shooter's father in his arms, reportedly for as long as an hour, to comfort him. Many of the members of the Amish community attended the funeral of the shooter and invited his widow to the funeral of one of the victims ("Among the Amish, a Grace That Endures," *Philadelphia Inquirer).*

She responded with an open letter to her Amish neighbors thanking them for their forgiveness, grace, and mercy. She wrote, "Your love for our family has helped to provide the healing we so desperately need. Gifts you've given touched our hearts in a way no words can describe. Your compassion has reached beyond our family, beyond our community, and is changing our world, and for this we sincerely thank you.

"Please know that our hearts have been broken by all that has happened. We are filled with sorrow for all of our Amish neighbors whom we have loved and continue to love. We know that there are many hard days ahead for all the families who lost loved ones, and so we will continue to put our hope and trust in the God of all comfort as we all seek to rebuild our lives." ("Amish Shooting Victims," www.800padutch.com/amishvictims.shtml.)

"There were some commentators who criticized the swift and complete forgiveness with which the Amish responded, arguing that forgiveness is inappropriate when no remorse has been expressed, and that such an attitude runs the risk of denying the existence of evil; others were supportive. Donald Kraybill and two other scholars of Amish life noted that 'letting go of grudges' is a deeply-rooted value in Amish culture...They explained that the Amish willingness to forgo vengeance does not undo the tragedy or pardon the wrong, but rather constitutes a first step toward a future that is more hopeful" (http://en.wikipedia.org/Amish_school_shooting).

The Christian acts of the Amish teach the therapeutic value of foregoing a grudge and forgiving those who have caused us grief and harm. The Sermon on the Mount teaches us that there is spiritual value as well. "Do good to them that hate you, and pray for them which despitefully use you." (Matthew 5:44)

6

PRIDE GOES BEFORE A FALL

"Opinion polls asking about the world's greatest problems often include responses such as the economy, disease, crime, political corruption, or the environment. According to the Book of Mormon, however, one of the world's main problems is an attitude best described as pride. In the Book of Mormon, pride seems to be the most individually and collectively destructive sin" (Byron R. Merrill, "They Wrote to Us As If We Were Present," *Ensign*, Jan 2000,13).

Many verses in the Old Testament speak of pride as well. "Pride goeth before destruction, and an haughty spirit before a fall" (Proverbs 16:18). "Talk no more so exceeding proudly; let not arrogancy come out of your mouth: for the Lord is a God of knowledge, and by him actions are weighed" (I Samuel 2:3). The Prophet Muhammad said, "He in whose heart there is as much as an atom of arrogance will not enter paradise." In Taoism, pride and greed are human errors, and the Roman Catholic Church lists pride as the most deadly of the seven deadly sins.

A History of Pride

There is ample evidence in the scriptures that demonstrates the consequences of pride to individuals, groups and entire nations. We often think of the destruction of Sodom and Gomorrah as a result of the sexual immorality of the people. Indeed, the Lord told Abraham of his need to destroy the cities, "Because the cry of Sodom and Gomorrah is great, and because their sin is very grievous" (Genesis 18:20). But we gain more insight into their sinful ways when the prophet Ezekiel speaks about the abominations of the people of Jerusalem. "Behold, this was the iniquity of thy sister Sodom, pride, fullness of bread, and abundance of idleness was in her and in her daughters, neither did she strengthen the hand of the poor and needy. And they were haughty, and committed abomination before me: therefore I took them away as I saw good" (Ezekiel 16:49-50).

This seems to indicate that the pride of the people brought about such conditions that led to their refusal to accept good over evil. Just as envy can lead one to commit sins of destruction, so pride and haughtiness can lead to wickedness with the likes of Sodom and Gomorrah. It is as St. Thomas Aquinas wrote, "Inordinate self-love is the cause of every sin."

As Jesus went on his way to Bethany, a town not far from Jerusalem, he was met by Martha. She and her sister Mary were grieved that their brother, Lazarus had died and that Jesus had not been there earlier to heal him. But Jesus called forth Lazarus and he rose from the dead. Some of the people who surrounded the tomb believed in the healing power of Jesus and in his words. However, some went to the Pharisees and told them of the miracles that had been performed and that this man had claimed to be the Son of God (John 11: 1-46).

Then we see how pride controlled the thoughts and actions of these men who felt a threat to their power and position. "If we let him thus alone, all men will believe on him: and the Romans shall come and take away both our place and nation. Then from that day forth they took counsel together for to put him to death" (John 11:48, 53).

The Book of Mormon contains a history of the Nephite people that becomes an almost predictable pattern. This "pride cycle" is apparent throughout the entire book of scripture, but is especially vivid in the books of Alma and Helaman. With the Lord as their guide, the Nephites became a great and prosperous nation. In spite of the fact they had encountered many wars and contentions with the Lamanites, and some had become hardened, their leaders continued to fortify them with the word of God. "And the people of Nephi began to prosper again in the land, and began to multiply and to wax exceedingly strong again in the land. And they began to grow exceedingly rich. But notwithstanding their riches, or their strength, or their prosperity, they were not lifted up in their pride of their eyes; neither were they slow to remember the Lord their God; but they did humble themselves exceedingly before him" (Alma 62:48-49).

This, then, is the first stage of the pride cycle, righteousness and prosperity. This is a state of richness that all nations and all families and all individuals would like to enjoy. But we can learn from the examples of the Nephites how pride can seep into the threads of our weaknesses until it tears us apart from our bond with God and unravels into wickedness. "And in the fifty and first year of the reign of the judges there was peace also, save it were the pride which began to enter into the church—not the church of God, but into the hearts of the people who professed to belong to the church of God. And they were lifted up in pride, even to the persecution of many of their brethren. Now this was a great evil, which did cause the more humble part of the people to suffer great persecutions, and to wade through much affliction" (Helaman 3:33-34). The second stage of the pride cycle has now begun with pride and wickedness.

As contention continues in the land, Nephite dissenters and the Lamanites join forces and take over some of the Nephite cities. The Nephites suffer many defeats "... because of the pride of their hearts, because of their exceeding riches, yea, it was because of their oppression to the poor, withholding their food from the hungry, withholding their clothing from the naked, and smiting their humble brethren upon the cheek, making a mock of that which was sacred, denying the spirit of prophecy and of revelation, murdering, plundering, lying, stealing, committing adultery, rising up in great contentions, and deserting away into the land of Nephi, among the Lamanites" (Helaman 4:12).

Many of the Nephites were deceived by the Gadianton robbers and allowed them to take over the Nephite government. "Satan did stir up the hearts of the more part of the Nephites, insomuch that they did unite with those bands of robbers, and did enter into their covenants and their oaths..." (Helaman 6:21). Nephi and Lehi, sons of Helaman, were grieved because of the iniquity of the Nephites and took it upon themselves to devote the rest of their lives to preaching the word of God among all the people in the Nephite cities. From there, they continued on to preach among the Lamanites. Because the Nephites were still hardening their hearts, and the Lamanites were beginning to heed the word of the Lord, "the Lamanites had become, the more part of them, a righteous people, insomuch that their righteousness did exceed that of the Nephites, because of their firmness and their steadiness in the faith" (Helaman 6:1). "And thus we see that the Nephites did begin to dwindle in unbelief, and grow in wickedness and abominations, while the Lamanites began to grow exceedingly in the knowledge of their God"...(Helaman 6:34).

Because of the Nephite wickedness and the contentions that increased, the people experienced much devastation and suffering. Many were destroyed in the wars that were all through the land. Nephi feared that they would be utterly destroyed and went to the Lord to plead for his people. "Oh Lord, do not suffer that this people shall be destroyed by the sword; but O Lord, rather let there be a famine in the land, to stir them up in remembrance of the Lord their God, and perhaps they will repent and turn unto thee" (Helaman 11:4).

"And so it was done, according to words of Nephi. And there was a great famine upon the land, among all the people...the earth was smitten that it was dry, and did not yield forth grain in the season of grain" and the people were "smitten that they did perish by the thousands in the more wicked parts of the land" (Helaman 11:5, 6). And thus we see the third part of the pride cycle, that of destruction and suffering.

Not until the people of Nephi suffered for several years from the famine did they begin to humble themselves and look to God again for strength. "And it came to pass that the people saw that they were about to perish by famine, and they began to remember the Lord their God..." (Helaman 11:7). When Nephi saw that the people were humble and repented, he asked the Lord again to bring rain, allow the crops to grow and spare the people from death. This was done and the people rejoiced and glorified God and esteemed Nephi as a great prophet. Peace came to the people and the church spread throughout the land (Helaman 11:8-21). The pride cycle is completed by the humility and repentance of the people.

However, because this is indeed a cycle, we find that righteousness and prosperity lasted only a few years before "they began again to forget the Lord their God" and "wax strong in iniquity" and "wax stronger and stronger in their pride, and in their wickedness; and thus they were ripening again for destruction" (Helaman 11: 36, 37).

Elder M. Russell Ballard said, "You don't have to be a Latter-day Saint—you don't even have to be religious—to see the repeating pattern of history in the lives of God's children as recorded in the Old Testament. Time and time again we see the cycle of righteousness followed by wickedness. Similarly, the Book of Mormon records that ancient civilization of this continent followed exactly the same pattern: righteousness followed by prosperity, followed by material comforts, followed by greed, followed by pride, followed by wickedness and a collapse of morality until the people brought calamities upon themselves sufficient to stir them up to humility, repentance, and change. In the relatively short span of years covered by the New Testament, the historic pattern repeats itself again. This time the people turned against Christ and His Apostles. The collapse was so great we have come to know it as the Great Apostasy, which led to the centuries of spiritual stagnation and ignorance called the Dark Ages ("Learning the Lessons of the Past," *Liahona*, May 2009, 32).

When I read such examples, I can't help but want to shout, "Don't you people get it! Can't you see what is going to happen?" But one only needs to examine the history of other great nations to see that we don't always "get it." Destruction has come upon these nations when their ease of life and their richness allows them to forget from whence the riches have come. In a challenging speech titled "Who Is Tampering with the Soul of America?" Jenkin Lloyd Jones said the pathway of history is littered with the bones of dead states and fallen empires. He points out that "Rome did not fall because its walls were low, but because Rome itself was low." The sensuality, orgies, and gradually weakened fiber of a once self-disciplined people brought Rome down. (Speech first delivered to the Inland Daily Press Association, Chicago, 1962).

In 1831, Alexis Tocqueville went to the United States at the request of his French Government. He studied the political system, the penal institutions and examined the country's social institutions. His studies culminated in a four-volume work titled, *Democracy in America*. He explains his findings when he observes, "I sought for the greatness and genius of America in her commodious harbors and her ample rivers, and it was not there; in her fertile and boundless prairies, and it was not there; in her rich mines and her vast world commerce, and it was not there. Not until I went to the churches of America and heard her pulpits aflame with righteousness did I understand the secret of her genius and power. America is great because she is good, and if America ever ceases to be good, America will cease to be great."

The prosperity and freedoms and richness of America have been a well-respected fact. However, if the people of America and other free and prosperous nations follow the pattern that led to the downfall of previous great people and nations, their prosperity can be killed by pride faster than from war-like attacks.

There is a quote attributed to George Santayana, "Those who cannot remember the past are condemned to repeat it" (*The Life of Reason*, Vol. 1, 1905). Our prosperous nations must learn from the past and its prophetic history so that the pride of our hearts does not lull us into a false sense of security.

The Heart of Pride

If we examine the meaning of pride, we will find in the Merriam-Webster Dictionary these rather conflicting definitions: a) reasonable or justifiable self-respect, b) delight or elation arising from some act, possession, or relationship, c) inordinate self-esteem: conceit. It would appear that on one level, pride is a positive expression or appreciation of self, possessions or relationships. At another level, however, pride is arrogant and boastful. If it is indeed both of these, pride is essentially an attitude of the heart. It is how we feel in our hearts that contributes to pride and joy, or to pride and sin.

A mother was telling of attending her youngest daughter's wedding in the temple. She spoke of the joy she had as she looked around the sealing room and recognizing that "all her children were together with her in the temple that day." She was visibly humbled by that blessing and said she mentioned it not out of boasting but out of thankfulness. It was the attitude in her heart that allowed her comment to be heard and felt as an expression of gratitude rather than conceited pride.

This type of pride, sometimes termed by psychologists as alpha pride, concerns feelings of inward gratification and a pleasant emotion. It could follow a goal that had been accomplished. It could be the feeling that results from making healthier choices or of providing more service to others or taking care of our homes and families. We take pride in a job well done. We take pride in our country and in our culture.

By contrast, beta pride, or hubris, as the Ancient Greeks termed it, has a negative connotation. It can be related to vanity, an arrogant tone, or expressions of aggression and hostility. Hubris also refers to conflicts of man against their fellow man and is used to describe those who considered themselves to be more important than the gods.

I am intrigued by the powerful messages concerning pride in the short story, "The Scarlet Ibis." James Hurst explores the conflict between the positive nature of pride and the consequences when pride is self-serving.

Even at his birth, the parents of William Armstrong, later nicknamed Doodle, make preparations for his death. He is an invalid and not expected to live. Doodle's older brother, embarrassed by Doodle's limitations, refuses to accept them and is determined to teach him to walk. Although Doodle sees no reason to conform, Brother is insistent. The fact that Brother chooses to help Doodle become stronger and accomplish new skills is admirable. The *motivation behind his efforts* is what twists that sense of pride into a scourge.

After much practicing, and on the chosen day, Brother surprised the family by revealing how Doodle could walk by himself to his chair at the dining room table. When Doodle said it was Brother who taught him how to walk, the family hugged Brother and praised him. This caused some tears on Brother's part because, "They did not know that I did it for myself; that pride, whose slave I was, spoke to me louder than all their voices and that Doodle walked only because I was ashamed of having a crippled brother."

That did not stop Brother, however. He began to believe in his own infallibility, and prepared a regimented training program for Doodle. He knew that it was perhaps too strenuous for Doodle's weak body, "But all of us must have something to be proud of, and Doodle had become mine." In the end, Brother's attempts to push Doodle further, fail to yield the hoped-for results and ultimately contribute to Doodle's death. We may reflect on this aspect of pride as Brother does when he says, "I did not know then that pride is a wonderful, terrible thing, a seed that bears two vines, life and death" (*The Atlantic Monthly*, 1960).

That wonderful vine of pride allowed Doodle to experience a life outside his bed and progress beyond his own imagination. Out of that same pride arose another vine, bitter and selfish, causing destruction and death. As Brother said, "All of us must have something to be proud of."

At the same time, we must examine our motivation, being careful not to fall into the trap of boastful arrogance. Clarifying these differences is important in clarifying the heart of pride.

One of the best sources for understanding the very core and nature of pride is in President Ezra Taft Benson's message to the April 1989 general conference. "Most of us think of pride as self-centeredness, conceit, boastfulness, arrogance, or haughtiness. All of these are elements of the sin, but the heart, or core, is still missing. The central feature of pride is enmity–enmity toward God and enmity toward our fellowmen. Enmity means 'hatred toward, hostility to, or a state of opposition.' It is the power by which Satan wishes to reign over us.

"Pride is essentially competitive in nature. We pit our will against God's. When we direct our pride toward God, it is in the spirit of 'my will and not thine be done.' As Paul said, they 'seek their own, not the things which are Jesus Christ's' (Phillipians 2:21). Our will in competition to God's will allow desires, appetites, and passions to go unbridled. The proud cannot accept the authority of God giving direction to their lives. They pit their perceptions of truth against God's great knowledge, their abilities versus God's priesthood power, their accomplishments against His mighty works."

"Our enmity toward God takes on many labels, such as rebellion, hard-heartedness, stiff-neckedness, unrepentant, puffed up, easily offended, and sign seekers. The proud wish God would agree with them. They aren't interested in changing their opinions to agree with God's" ("Beware of Pride," *Ensign*, May 1984, 4). What a perfect description for defining what is actually taking place in our hearts when we are prideful!

If pride is "enmity toward God and our fellowman," it is in direct opposition to the first two commandments: "Thou shalt love the Lord thy God with all they heart, and with all thy soul and with all thy mind," and "Thou shalt love thy neighbor as thyself" (Matthew 22:37-39). When examined in this way, it is understandable how far one can get from what is god-like when filled with an attitude of pride.

One example of how pride is puffed up and will not allow us to change our opinions is in the story of a ship's captain. "One night at sea, this captain saw what looked like the light of another ship heading toward him. He had his signalman blink to the other ship: 'Change your course 10 degrees south.' The reply came back, 'Change *your* course 10 degrees north.' The ship's captain answered: 'I am a captain. Change *your* course south.' To which the reply came, 'Well, I am a seaman first class. Change *your* course north.' This so infuriated the captain, he signaled back, 'I say change *your* course south. I am on a battleship!' To which the reply came back, 'And I say change *your* course north. I am in a lighthouse.' Like the captain, if we fail to modify our course and purge ourselves of pride, we may find ourselves shipwrecked upon the shoals of life..." (H. David Burton, "Courage to Hearken," *Ensign*, May 1994, 66).

Forms of Pride

While the scriptures abound with examples of pride, we can easily observe the forms of pride that exist in ourselves and in those with whom we associate. Sadly, there is ample evidence of those who have attempted to elevate themselves above their neighbor. We sometimes call it, "Keeping up with the Jones's." It is as if a competition is taking place but no one is winning. In the words of C.S. Lewis: "Pride gets no pleasure out of having something, only out of having more of it than the next man... It is the comparison that makes you proud: the pleasure of being above the rest. Once the element of competition has gone, pride has gone" (*Mere Christianity*, New York: Macmillan, 1952, 109-110).

I recall a few years ago driving around some neighborhoods and curious as to what these people did for a living in order to afford such large and magnificent homes. My husband indicated that maybe they really couldn't afford them. That seemed incomprehensible to me at the time. But I later took note of the economic situation with some of those same houses in foreclosure. While many were adjusting their lifestyle to fit their new wage situation, many were not, and were finding themselves in an extreme amount of personal debt, one of the predictors of a recession. "Some prideful people are not so concerned as to whether their wages meet their needs as they are that their wages are more than someone else's. Their reward is being a cut above the rest. This is the enmity of pride" (Ezra Taft Benson, "Beware of Pride," *Ensign*, May 1984, 4).

Prideful people desire "the praise of men more than the praise of God" (John 12:43).

Another form of pride is intellectual pride. "Intellectual pride is very prevalent in our day. Some people exalt themselves above God and His anointed servants because of their learning and scholarly achievements. We must never allow our intellect to take priority over our spirit. Our intellect can feed our spirit and our spirit can feed our intellect, but if we allow our intellect to take precedence over our spirit, we will stumble, find fault, and may even lose our testimonies. Knowledge is very important and one of the few things that accompanies us into the next life. We should always be learning. However, we must be careful not to set aside our faith in the process, because faith actually enhances our ability to learn" (Joseph B. Wirthlin, "Press On," *Liahona*, Nov 2004, 101–104).

As I visited with a young woman in our ward one day, the conversation turned to what she had been reading. She indicated that she had just read a rather disturbing article in a newspaper. It concerned a former ward bishop who had also done some scientific research into the DNA of early settlers on the American continent. Because of his research, he questioned the veracity of the Book of Mormon. This young woman then said in exasperation, "He should know better than that!" We all should know better than to think our "vast" amount of knowledge could be more than God's.

Jacob recognized the source of such intellectual pride when he stated, "O that cunning plan of the evil one! O the vainness, and the frailties, and the foolishness of men! When they are learned they think they are wise, and they hearken not unto the counsel of God, for they set it aside, supposing they know of themselves, wherefore, their wisdom is foolishness and it profiteth them not. But to be learned is good if they hearken unto the counsels of God" (2 Ne. 9:28-29).

We admire those whose intellect allows them to teach, lead, research and inspire. However, we should never allow our intellect to take precedence over our spiritual foundation or our appointed leaders. We can never substitute our own knowledge for the prophesies and revelations received from God, and we should never be deceived by those who do so. Christ warned us, "Beware of false prophets, which come to you in sheep's clothing, but inwardly they are ravening wolves" (Matt. 7:15).

Those who hold grudges because of a real or perceived offense are actually exhibiting pride. Their pride will not allow them to return to activity, or acknowledge authority, receive council or forgive another. Mistakes are often made by the "natural man" who administers in the Church, but that does not mean the Church is untrue. The principles and blessings remain the same. Those who choose to be offended in this way miss those blessings.

Many are familiar with the example of Thomas B. Marsh. Marsh was the first President of the Quorum of the Twelve Apostles and held the responsibility of leading the Twelve in their mission to preach the Gospel to the world. He gave much of his time and effort for the building up of the Church. However, an unfortunate incident between his wife, Elizabeth and a Sister Harris, created such pride in his heart, that he later apostatized.

"While the Saints were in Far West, Missouri, Elizabeth Marsh, Thomas's wife, and her friend Sister Harris decided they would exchange milk in order to make more cheese than they otherwise could. To be certain all was done fairly, they agreed that they should not save what were called the strippings, but that the milk and strippings should all go together. Strippings came at the end of the milking and were richer in cream.

"Sister Harris was faithful to the agreement, but Sister Marsh, desiring to make some especially delicious cheese, saved a pint of strippings from each cow and sent Sister Harris the milk without the strippings. This caused the two women to quarrel. When they could not settle their differences, the matter was referred to the home teachers to settle. They found Elizabeth Marsh guilty of failure to keep her agreement. She and her husband were upset with the decision, and the matter was then referred to the bishop for a Church trial. The bishop's court decided that the strippings were wrongfully saved and that Sister Marsh had violated her covenant with Sister Harris.

"Thomas Marsh appealed to the high council, and the men comprising this council confirmed the bishop's decision. He then appealed to the First Presidency of the Church. Joseph Smith and his counselors considered the case and upheld the decision of the high council.

"Elder Thomas B. Marsh, who sided with his wife through all of this, became angrier with each successive decision-so angry, in fact, that he went before a magistrate and swore that the Mormons were hostile toward the state of Missouri. His affidavit led to-or at least was a factor in-Governor Lilburn Boggs's cruel extermination order, which resulted in over 15,000 Saints being driven from their homes, with all the terrible suffering and consequent death that followed. All of this occurred because of a disagreement over the exchange of milk and cream.

"After 19 years of rancor and loss, Thomas B. Marsh made his way to the Salt Lake Valley and asked President Brigham Young for forgiveness. Brother Marsh also wrote to Heber C. Kimball, First Counselor in the First Presidency, of the lesson he had learned. Said Brother Marsh: 'The Lord could get along very well without me and He ... lost nothing by my falling out of the ranks; But O what have I lost! Riches, greater riches than all this world or many planets like this could afford' (Thomas S. Monson, "School Thy Feelings, O My Brother," *Liahona*, Nov 2009, 62, 67–69).

Another incident in our Church History illustrating how offenses can fester and pride can result is in the example of the dedication of the Kirtland Temple. After the temple was completed, many of the Saints gathered for its dedication. However, not everyone could be seated inside the building because it filled so quickly with those anxious to attend. One who was not allowed into the building was Elder Frazier Eaton. He had arrived after the seats were taken and no standing room was left. The dedication was repeated the next day for those who could not be accommodated the first day, but Frazier Eaton, who had given $700 for the building of the temple, was offended and as a result, apostatized (See George A. Smith, in *Journal of Discourses,* 11:9).

While these examples cause us to wonder at the improbable decisions made by these men, we should examine our own decisions that are often a result of our pride. Do we think serving in the Nursery is beneath us? Do we choose not to attend a meeting because of the notion that we don't "fit in?" Do we obey only the commandments that seem sensible to us and ignore the others? Do we choose not to forgive, even though we are "required to forgive all men?" (D&C 64:10) Do we become defensive when we are corrected by our leaders? "When pride has a hold on our hearts, we lose our independence of the world and deliver our freedoms to the bondage of men's judgment. The world shouts louder than the whisperings of the Holy Ghost. The reasoning of men overrides the revelations of God, and the proud let go of the iron rod" (Ezra Taft Benson, "The Faces of Pride," *New Era*, Oct 2003, 40).

Other forms of pride include faultfinding and gossiping. President Benson explains how this is a common practice today. "Pride is a sin that can readily be seen in others but is rarely admitted in ourselves. Most of us consider pride to be a sin of those on the top, such as the rich and the learned, looking down at the rest of us. There is, however, a far more common ailment among us–that is pride from the bottom looking up. It is manifested in so many ways, such as faultfinding, gossiping, backbiting, murmuring, living beyond our means, envying, coveting, withholding gratitude and praise that might lift another, and being unforgiving and jealous" (Ezra Taft Benson, "The Faces of Pride," *New Era*, Oct 2003, 40).

I have experienced several conversations with teenagers that exhibit this form of pride. This is a typical example:

"I hate those preppies. They think they're so cool."

"Which one?"

"All of them."

"Has someone in particular said or done something to offend you?"

"No, but they're all alike. They just think they're all that with their cutesy clothes and their perfect lives. They never talk to me or sit by me."

"Maybe they're shy or maybe they feel intimidated by you."

"Oh, yeah, right!"

"Have you ever talked to one of them or sat by them?"

"No! I can't stand them."

This type of pride is a definite ailment among our young people. The act of judging, being jealous and finding fault, especially with no concrete evidence to support their bias, is an everyday occurrence. It infiltrates schools, sabotages unity and fuels fights. It impedes the progress of both parties to work toward a common goal. We may consider these attitudes as a "part of life," a "right of passage" that will go away once one reaches adulthood. But do they? Has there ever been an adult who has judged an entire group of people on what he perceives the people to be, never having known one personally? Has there ever been a nation who hates another nation because of its "status" and seeks to pull it down?

It is certain that the simple act of reaching the age of an adult is no cure for pride, jealousy and faultfinding. Maturity must attend adulthood, wisdom must temper bias, and humility must enter our hearts and souls. Indeed, if there is an antidote for the disease of pride, it is humility.

Antidote for Pride

In C.S. Lewis' book, *The Screwtape Letters*, Wormwood, a young demon and nephew to Screwtape, is being tutored by the senior demon. Screwtape advises his nephew in the form of letters that contain advice for how to turn Wormwood's "Patient" toward "Our Father Below" (Satan) and away from "the Enemy" (God).

Eventually, Wormwood gets the jist of his occupation and wishes to tempt his patient into extravagantly wicked and deplorable sins. Screwtape, on the other hand, is not interested in getting the patient to commit anything spectacularly evil, saying that "the safest path to hell is the gradual one." And then we gain even more insight into the intricate workings of pride when Screwtape mentions to his apprentice, "Your patient has become humble; have you drawn his attention to that fact?" (*The Screwtape Letters*, 1982, 62-63)

Screwtape was aware that humility would conquer the patient's pride and therefore turn the patient's focus to "the Enemy." In reality, Satan is aware of man's weaknesses as well. He knows that he can gradually lead us away from God by tossing pride into our path and watching gleefully from the gutter as we stumble. After that, he doesn't have to work very diligently to cause us to commit anything tremendously evil. However, if we become humble, his work becomes threatened.

"Pride is the universal sin, the great vice...The antidote for pride is humility–meekness, submissiveness. God will have a humble people. Either we can choose to be humble or we can be compelled to be humble" (Ezra Taft Benson, "Beware of Pride," *Ensign*, May 1989, 4).

In November of 2000, then President Hinckley addressed the youth of the church, offering them prayer and counsel in the form of the "Six B's". One of those B's was to "be humble." He presented these wise words, " There is no place for arrogance in our lives. There is no place for conceit. There is no place for egotism. We have a great work to do. We have things to accomplish. We need direction in the pursuit of our education. We need help in choosing an eternal companion. The Lord has said, 'Be thou humble; and the Lord thy God shall lead thee by the hand, and give thee answer to thy prayers'" (D&C 112:10).

"What a tremendous promise is given in this statement. If we are without conceit and pride and arrogance, if we are humble and obedient, then the Lord will lead us by the hand and answer our prayers. What greater thing could we ask for? There is nothing to compare with this."

Some may mistake meekness for weakness, submissiveness for servitude, and humility for subservience. I recall being conflicted with that idea as well. I was just embarking on my college career when Helen Reddy debuted her song, "I Am Woman." There were lyrics that were equivalent to an anthem for females everywhere: "I am wise. I am strong. I am invincible. You can bend but never break me 'cause it only serves to make me more determined to achieve my final goal." I was thoroughly convinced.

At that same time, I was taking a Book of Mormon class and reading in the book of Mosiah. A particular scripture seemed to stand in direct conflict to Ms. Reddy's stirring lyrics. I focused on particular words and phrases: "the natural man is an enemy to God and has been from the fall of Adam and will be forever and ever...[until he] becometh as a child, submissive, meek...willing to submit to all things...even as a child doth submit to the will of his father" (Mosiah 3:19).

But I was not meek and submissive! I was strong! I was invincible! I was a roaring woman determined to raise my voice and achieve my goals! I was going to be assertive, and competitive. I was not only going to swim with the sharks, I was going to reel one in, bring it home and fry it up in a pan.

I completely misunderstood.

When I finally chose to ponder the whole scripture, I could better determine that humility was definitely not a weakness or a lack of power. "Natural man is an enemy to God...unless he yields to the enticings of the Holy Spirit...and becometh a saint through the atonement of Christ the Lord... and becometh humble, patient, [and] full of love..." (Mosiah 3:19). Having humility allows one to be teachable, accept correction, and feel gratitude. Yielding to the Holy Spirit and accepting the Lord's commands requires great strength.

The English author John Ruskin said, "The first test of a truly great man is his humility. By humility I don't mean doubt of his powers or hesitation in speaking his opinion, but merely an understanding of the relationship of what he can say and what he can do" (Quotations Book.

com). I would submit that we need also to have an understanding of our relationship with Christ in order to be truly great and truly humble.

Not only would humility help each person to be greater, it would change the climate of families and communities in a more positive way. "I think sometimes of what life would be like if we all possessed greater humility...Consider the climate that would exist within a marriage or family–or any organization, for that matter if through genuine humility mistakes were freely admitted and forgiven, if we were not afraid to praise others for fear they might gain on us...Contemplate the advantages of life in a society in which considerations of status were only secondary, where citizens were more concerned with their responsibilities than their rights and where those in authority might even occasionally step forward and humbly acknowledge, "I could have been wrong" (Marlin K. Jensen, "To Walk Humbly with Thy God," *Liahona*, July 2001, 11).

Whether our lumps are created from a combination of guilt and pride, from carrying grudges, from too large a dose of perfectionism or any other negative habit, they can be "smoothed." These are not the only examples, however. There is procrastination, being prone to anger, being judgmental, gossip, and a host of other lumps of our own creation. These are the habits that keep us from really enjoying this mortal life and ultimately immortality. The good news is that with God's help, we can practically eliminate them from smothering the smooth goodness of all that is possible.

Sometimes there will be obstacles entering our path that are NOT of our own making. We need to fortify our resistance for those events as well. Strengthening our bodies, minds and spirits will allow us to indeed feel the fullness of joy that we seek. These next four chapters examine a few of those aspects:

7

IN GOD'S IMAGE

One of the messages we received at the Grand Council in Heaven was that the purpose for our progression was to have a fullness of joy. In order to do this, our spirits needed to be clothed with a physical body (D&C 93:30-34). The Family Proclamation states, "Spirit sons and daughters knew and worshipped God as their Eternal Father and accepted His plan by which His children could obtain a physical body and gain earthly experience to progress toward perfection and ultimately realize his or her divine destiny as an heir of eternal life."

We were privileged to learn that our bodies would be in the image of God. In fact, we shouted for joy when we learned of His plan of happiness (Job 38:7).

Be Grateful

We often take our bodies for granted. After all, they have been with us since we were born and before we even remember. They go with us wherever we go. They stare back at us through the mirror. Often, we grimace at the reflection that peers back at us. We find flaws in the way our hair curls, or doesn't curl, or if it has left our head altogether. We wish our noses were shaped differently, or our legs were longer or our waists were thinner. We often forget that it is a glorious creation worthy of our deepest gratitude.

President Russell M. Nelson, who was an internationally renowned surgeon and medical researcher, helps us understand its magnificence. He indicates that a study of the body attests to its divine creation. From its formation beginning with the union of two cells, to its defense, repair and regeneration, it functions "in a marvelous manner, beyond my ... ability to describe."

"Twenty-three chromosomes from each parent unite in one new cell. These chromosomes contain thousands of genes that determine all of the physical characteristics of the unborn person. Approximately 22 days after these two cells unite, a little heart begins to beat. At 26 days, blood begins to circulate. Cells multiply and divide, some to become eyes that see. Some become ears that hear, while others are destined to become fingers."

A good portion of President Nelson's life's study was focused on the heart. He describes it as "a jewel...a pump so magnificent that its power is almost beyond our comprehension. Four important valves, pliable as a parachute and delicate as a dainty silk scarf open and close over 100,000 times a day–over 36 million times a year to control the flow of blood. No man-made material developed thus far can be flexed so frequently and flow so long without breaking. Each day the heart pumps enough fluid to fill a 2,000-gallon tank. The work it performs daily is equivalent to lifting a 150-pound man to the top of the Empire State Building, while consuming less energy than that used by a small light bulb."

President Nelson continues to describe the marvels of the brain, the circulatory system, skin, body organs, self-defense mechanisms and self-repair and renewal. He reminds us that many have tried to explain our existence by saying we were formed out of nothing or from organic evolution or that the universe began as a "big bang" that resulted in the creation of our planet and life upon it.

"To me, such theories are unbelievable! Could an explosion in a printing shop produce a dictionary? It is unthinkable! Even if it could be argued to be within a remote realm of possibility, such a dictionary could certainly not heal its own torn pages or renew its own worn corners or reproduce its own subsequent editions! We are children of God, created by him and formed in his image." (address delivered at Brigham Young University, March 29, 1987)

I love being a grandmother. It is a privilege and a delight! It is difficult to express the joy and gratitude felt while witnessing a new life emerge with his or her distinctive characteristics from each parent. When each little child was born with all fingers, toes and all organs functioning properly, it was a spiritual experience. We knew we were in the presence of a celestial spirit that now had a perfect physical body. How can we not be grateful for such a marvelous creation and gift?

It is easy to celebrate new life and the magnificence of its mortal package. As our bodies age, however, we tend to forget its value and begin to complain of its flaws. Susan W. Tanner expressed her concern about obvious physical flaws during her adolescent years. "I remember well the insecurities I felt as a teenager with a bad case of acne. I tried to care for my skin properly. My parents helped me get medical attention. For years, I even went without eating chocolate and all the greasy foods around which teens often socialize, but with no obvious healing consequences. It was difficult for me at that time to fully appreciate this body which was giving me so much grief. But my good mother taught me a higher law. Over and over she said to me, 'You must do everything you can to make your appearance pleasing, but the minute you walk out the door, forget yourself and start concentrating on others'" (Susan W. Tanner, "The Sanctity of the Body," *Liahona*, Nov. 2005, 14).

I enjoy the poem, "Phizzog," by Carl Sandburg that has similar instruction. It acknowledges that our physical package was a gift to us and, in spite of how we view it, it is our duty to do something constructive with it.

This face you got.

This here phizzog you carry around,

You never picked it out for yourself, at all, at all–did you?

This here phizzog–somebody handed it to you–am I right?

Somebody said, "Here's yours, now go see what you can do with it."

Somebody slipped it to you and it was like a package marked:

"No goods exchanged after being taken away"

This face you got.

(From *Good Morning, America*, 1928)

"For reasons usually unknown, some people are born with physical limitations. Specific parts of the body may be abnormal. Regulatory systems may be out of balance. And all of our bodies are subject to disease and death. Nevertheless, the gift of a physical body is priceless. A perfect body is not required to achieve a divine destiny. In fact, some of the sweetest spirits are housed in frail frames. Great spiritual strength is often developed by those with physical challenges precisely because they are challenged. Such individuals are entitled to all the blessings that God has in store for His faithful and obedient children" (Russell M. Nelson, "You Are a Chid of God," *New Era*, Jul 2008).

President Boyd K. Packer found himself in a situation that caused him concern about his physical abilities. Because of childhood polio, he was not able to participate in sports and was left with a feeling of inferiority when compared to his friends. But his patriarchal blessing gave him great comfort. In it, he was told this: "You made a free and willing decision to abide by the laws of Eternal Progress as outlined by our elder brother, the Lord Jesus Christ. You...have been...given a physical body with which you might experience Earth Life...a body of such physical proportions and fitness as to enable your spirit to function through it unhampered by physical impediments...Cherish this as a great heritage" (patriarchal blessing of Boyd K. Packer, 15 Jan. 1944, 1).

We should all cherish the blessing of a physical body. And when we feel frail, when we feel that our body impedes our progress, we can take comfort in the knowledge that the time will come when each "soul shall be restored to the body, and the body to the soul; yea, and every limb and joint shall be restored to its body; yea, even a hair of the head shall not be lost; but all things shall be restored to their proper and perfect frame" (Alma 40:23).

Respect It

I recently had occasion to visit with two different women who held the same position in their place of business. Each was in an office and was the supervisor of catering and hospitality for their hotel. The woman at the first hotel was well groomed, dressed in a professional-looking suit, stood up and addressed me as I entered the room and took time to answer my questions cheerfully and respectfully. The woman at the second hotel, while youthful and attractive, was dressed in casual jeans, remained in her desk and handed me a sheet of paper with information.

Although these encounters were brief, I felt I had received a great amount of information. The message I received from the first woman was that she respected herself and her position. I gathered that she would do her best to organize the occasion and take care of my needs. Because of the casual dress and attitude of the second woman, I was given the impression that she didn't care about either her job or whether I scheduled a function at her hotel. This may not have been the case, but that's the message I received from the body language. Although the venue and prices for food were equal, I chose the first.

While neither of these women was immodestly dressed, their attire and behavior still sent a message. Clothing can influence our actions and the way others act towards us. Our outward appearance often reflects what will be found on the inside. If we respect our bodies, we will be in command of our appearance.

President Harold B. Lee taught of the important symbolic and actual effect of how we dress and groom our bodies. "If you are well groomed and modestly dressed, you invite the companionship of the

Spirit of our Father in Heaven and exercise a wholesome influence upon those around you. To be unkempt in your appearance exposes you to influences that are degrading" (*The Teachings of Harold B. Lee*, ed. Clyde J. Williams 220).

A message in *True to the Faith* continues to give understanding to respecting our bodies. "Prophets have always counseled us to dress modestly. This truth is founded on the truth that the human body is God's sacred creation. Respect your body as a gift from God.

"Like your dress and grooming, your language and behavior are expressions of your character. Your words and actions can have a profound influence on you and on others. Express yourself through clean, positive, uplifting language and in actions that bring happiness to those around you. Your efforts to be modest in word and deed lead to increased guidance and comfort from the Holy Ghost.

"Avoid the filthy language and the casual, irreverent use of the Lord's name that are so common in the world. Withstand any temptation to participate in extreme or inappropriate behavior. The irreverent nature of such language and behavior impairs your ability to receive the quiet promptings of the Holy Ghost" (*True to the Faith*, pg. 107).

There is a story told of a woman who was having gall bladder surgery. During that process, her spirit left and went to the Pearly Gates. Saint Peter looked at the records and said, "You're not supposed to be here now. You have 20 more years left on earth. You need to go back." After that revealing incident she decided that if she had twenty more years with that body, she might as well spruce it up a little. She decided she would have several plastic surgeries–some augmentation here, some liposuction there, some lifting elsewhere. She also had a large tattoo scrawled across her lower back and one around her ankle. In addition to her already pierced ears she added a nose piercing and one on her lip. As she walked out of the tattoo parlor with her final addition, she was hit by a truck, died, and went back to the pearly gates. Immediately she started questioning St. Peter, "I thought I had twenty more years!

What am I doing here? St. Peter gave her another look and said, "Oh! I'm sorry. I didn't recognize you!"

While the story may be fictitious, it does bring us to question how our Lord would feel if we defiled the body that was given to us with tattoos and body piercing and unnecessary surgical procedures. And yet, we don't need to wonder. It is spelled out for us in the scriptures and spoken of by the prophets.

"Latter-day prophets strongly discourage the tattooing of the body and the piercing of the body ... If girls or women desire to have their ears pierced, they are encouraged to wear only one pair of modest earrings. Those who choose to disregard this counsel show a lack of respect for themselves and for God" (*True to the Faith*, p. 10).

The Apostle Paul taught of the significance of our bodies and the danger of purposefully defiling them: "Know ye not that ye are the temple of God, and that the Spirit of God dwelleth in you? If any man defile the temple of God, him shall God destroy, for the temple of God is holy, which temple ye are" (1 Corinthians 3:16-17).

Being in command of our appearance and our language shows respect for our bodies. Choosing not to defile the external surface of our bodies with tattoos and piercings is one way to observe this fact. It is the same principle that guides the construction of temples. Consider the outward appearance of each temple. The structure itself is always aesthetically pleasing and well constructed. Landscaping is arranged in a manner that adds to the inviting atmosphere. Flowers, trees and grasses that represent the area are carefully placed and maintained. One would likely receive the impression that the inside would be equally clean, pleasant and beautiful and would be correct in the assumption. That same principle holds true for our physical bodies.

The Word of Wisdom in section 89 of the Doctrine and Covenants is straightforward and warns us of the physical dangers of harmful substances as well as the physical and spiritual consequences of their abuse. Specifically "wine or strong drink, tobacco and hot drinks" defined as tea and coffee, are mentioned. (D&C 89:5-9) It is interesting that the

Lord revealed this law to the Prophet Joseph Smith long before science supported its accuracy. A plethora of information now exists on the harmful effects of illegal drugs and the misuse of prescription drugs. It is taught in schools, given money and attention by legislators and advertised on billboards and through other media. The consequences of ignoring this valuable information will certainly take a negative toll on the health of the person using these substances. But these addictions have other far-reaching consequences.

"Each year tobacco use causes nearly 2.5 million premature deaths worldwide. Tobacco use also harms millions of innocent victims. For example, smoking by pregnant mothers passes on toxic chemicals that interfere with fetal development, affecting approximately 3 million babies each year. Other innocent victims include nonsmokers who regularly inhale secondhand smoke. These people have much higher rates of respiratory illness and are three times more likely to die of lung cancer than those who do not inhale secondhand smoke. Smokeless tobacco is just as addictive as cigarettes, and users of smokeless tobacco have cancer rates up to fifty times higher than those who do not use tobacco" (See James O. Mason, "I Have a Question," *Ensign*, Sept. 1986, 59-61).

The First Presidency declared: "Drunken with strong drink, men have lost their reason; their counsel has been destroyed; their judgment and vision are fled. ...Drink has brought more woe and misery, broken more hearts, wrecked more homes, committed more crimes, filled more coffins, than all the wars the world has suffered" (in Conference Report, Oct. 1942, 8).

Many athletes have served as heroes to young people. We all admire their talents and abilities and enjoy the sports in which they perform. We are in awe of those who participate in Olympic events and esteem them for their physical prowess. However, some athletes today sport several tattoos or endorse products that could be harmful to the body. Others have violated drug laws or engaged in other unlawful or immoral practices. While many can still be emulated for choosing what is good for their bodies, there are heroes that can be found in the scriptures as well. One of those heroes is Daniel of the Old Testament.

Daniel was born in Israel in a time when the country was being used as a battleground by two neighboring nations, Syria and Egypt. When Daniel was just a child, Nebuchadnezzar, king of Babylon, besieged Jerusalem, and took sacred vessels from the temple as part of his spoils. The king also desired to make his country stronger by bringing back certain hostages. He wanted all the "children in whom was no blemish, but well favoured and skillful in all wisdom, and cunning in knowledge, and understanding science, and such as had ability in them to stand in the king's palace, and whom they might teach the learning and the tongue of the Chaldeans" (Dan. 1:4). Daniel was one of those chosen to go to the palace as a slave of the king.

Shortly after being taken from his home, Daniel faced his first challenge from the king. He and the other young men with him were to eat the food the king apportioned them, consisting of meat and wine. Daniel had been taught well and knew certain foods would defile his body. He made a request of the prince that he not be required to eat the meat and drink the wine. He made a proposition to the prince that he would only eat the foods that he had been taught were good for him. He would do this for ten days and if after that time, his countenance was not fairer and appearance more healthy than all the rest, he would do as the king required. At the end of the allotted time period, Daniel was indeed strong in body and mind and the king found him to be "ten times better than all the magicians and astrologers that were in all his realm" (Daniel 1:20). Like Daniel, we may also be the recipients of health, wisdom and knowledge. We can run and not be weary; walk and not faint. And all that is required is obedience to that same commandment Daniel observed. (See D&C sec. 89:18-20)

There would be those who would argue that the Word of Wisdom lacks a list of modern-day beverages or newly created drugs, therefore giving them carte blanche status. To that, President Gordon B. Hinckley declared, "What a miserable excuse. There is likewise no mention of the hazards of diving into an empty swimming pool or of jumping from an overpass onto the freeway. But who doubts the deadly consequences of such? Common sense would dictate against such behavior ("The Scourge of Illicit Drugs," *Ensign*, Nov. 1989, 48).

Perhaps a way to assist us in measuring the merit or danger of a particular substance would be to note the wording in Section 89. The word *wholesome* is used to describe the herbs that God has ordained for our use, and we are further instructed to use all foods with *prudence.* (verses 10-11) We could ask ourselves: Would putting this substance into my body be *prudent*? Is this a *wholesome* drink? Using this testing method before ingesting anything, can assist us in making a healthier choice and abiding by the Word of Wisdom. And do we really need to be commanded in all things? " ...For he that is compelled in all things, the same is a slothful and not a wise servant..." (D&C 58: 26).

Obedience to the Word of Wisdom is not the only course to take for keeping one's body healthy. Sexual purity is important for our spiritual strength and is essential for our physical health. When I was a teenager, I rarely heard of sexually transmitted diseases. I learned of a few in health classes, but they seemed far removed from anyone I knew. I recognized how they were transmitted and understood that antibiotics were the cure for most all the cases. I was taught at home and in church that sexual relations were an expression of love between a husband and wife and that sexual sins defiled the power that God had given us to create life.

Twenty-five years later when I had teenagers of my own, I came to realize that the world had changed considerably. More diseases were evident and prevalent. HIV/AIDS became well known and even feared. And it was apparent that a dose of antibiotics was not curing these diseases. Now STDs are one of the most critical health challenges facing the nation. The Center for Disease Control estimates that there are 19 million new infections every year in the United States. They cost the U.S. health care system $17 billion every year–and cost individuals even more in immediate and life-long health consequences.

One of the most flagrant and nefarious sexually transmitted diseases that now affects our generation is the HPV virus. Approximately 20 million Americans are currently infected with HPV. Another 6 million people become newly infected each year. HPV is so common that at least 50% of sexually active men and women get it at some point in their lives. Each year, about 12,000 women get cervical cancer in the U.S. Almost all of these cancers are HPV-associated. (cdc.gov/std/stats10).

"The sacred powers of procreation are to be employed only between man and woman, lawfully wedded as husband and wife" ("The Family: A Proclamation to the World"). The wisdom in God's commandment to be sexually pure is more evident every day. Obeying these commandments keeps our body healthy and certainly shows our respect for this glorious miracle that we are.

A Well-Oiled Machine

Most of us consider our cars worthy of our time, attention and care. We get the oil changed at each 6,000 mile mark or the date on the sticker attached by the mechanic at the last lube shop. We are careful to get the tires rotated, fill the tank with the proper grade of gasoline and place the rubber mats on the floor during wintertime. We add the right lubricants, watch for the warning lights, wash and wax, and do all we can to keep the motor running and the battery charged. We try not to expose our cars to the elements or to careless parkers in the parking lot and we obey traffic signs in order to avoid collisions with other vehicles on the road.

We are similarly careful when it comes to the care of our pets. They are groomed, kept in when it is cold outside, fed the right food (it's even in the refrigeration department these days) and we take them out for exercise. We make certain they have enough water, sunshine and visits to the veterinarian. Some over-achieving pet owners even arrange for play dates.

Somehow, this type of care and concern doesn't always transfer to taking care of our own physical bodies. We also require maintenance, exercise, the right fuel, tune-ups, social contact and avoidance of exposure to certain elements. Our motors need to run and our batteries need to be charged. Unfortunately, we can't go to a store and buy new parts when our bodies wear out, and we can't replace them with newer models.

While there have been some modern medical advances that have allowed us to live longer and stronger, there is one preventive medicine that continues to lead the pack in its potency and effectiveness. The medicine is free of charge and has no negative side effects. It is easily accessed and can be used successfully by young and old alike. That "medicine" is exercise.

My undergraduate degree was in physical education. I worked out for the "fun" of it. I swam, danced, played on the field hockey team and enjoyed snow skiing and water-skiing. I played tennis and golf, and tried my hand at basketball and gymnastics. But that was forty years ago. I find now that the mind is willing but the body doesn't seem to appreciate or enjoy the intense workouts it used to receive. I have had to adjust.

Like many others, I have gone through periods when I searched earnestly for easy ways to maintain health without moving off the couch or reducing my chocolate chip cookie intake. I've been collecting exercise equipment since the 70's attempting to look like the gals on the advertisements. I tried to look like Jane Fonda when she first made her appearance in exercise leotards and leg warmers (which, by the way, have come back into style–again). I tested out mini trampolines. That worked for a while, but after three children I had to wear tummy control panty hose in order for my belly to bounce in the same vertical direction as my feet and head. Treadmills make me rather bored and terribly hungry. I start immediately craving Hostess Cupcakes. Swimming is good. At least you get to lie down while you do it. But the drawback these days is having to wear a swimsuit; i.e. varicose veins, cellulite. Bicycling isn't bad if you find a seat big enough to fit comfortably under yours, and walking is wonderful until that rash comes from your thighs rubbing together too many times. Oh, yes. I have heard and *used* all the excuses.

With all the access we have to walking paths, gymnasiums, biking trails, swimming pools, and exercise dvd's, just to name a few, our excuses couldn't hold a five pound hand weight. I became especially aware of that when reading the book, *Playing the Enemy*, by John Carlin. The book describes Nelson Mandela's improbable and brilliant campaign as the South African President to unify the nation through the game of rugby. That had been his dream for many years, including the twenty-seven years he spent in prison for anti-apartheid activism.

He had an exercise routine that he had begun when he was a lawyer and amateur boxer. He would run for an hour before sunrise. When he was sent to prison in 1964, he remained inside a tiny cell for 18 years. This would have been enough to discourage most people, but Nelson Mandela, knowing the benefits of keeping his body and spirit strong, would run in place every morning for an hour in the cell. In 1982, he was transferred to another prison where he shared a cell with four others. The cell was half the size of a tennis court, allowing him to run short, tight laps. Even after his release from prison at age seventy-one, he briskly walked every morning for an hour before daybreak. His example, especially in light of his circumstances, tends to make any excuse I can conjure up to be rather shallow.

All whining aside, I know without a doubt that exercise is indeed a healthy "medicine" and is essential for body and mind. Not all bodies require intense workouts, but all bodies require movement. There is some recent fascinating evidence that indicates even 30 minutes a day of walking can make phenomenal differences in one's overall health.

Dr. Michael Evans is a family physician and Associate Professor in the Departments of Family Medicine and Public Health at the University of Toronto. He researched preventative medicine in order to understand what medicine had the largest impact on the most people and made the most return on their investment. He came to the conclusion that the "medicine" was exercise, mostly walking. He discovered that those with knee arthritis reduced their rates of pain and disability by 47% when using this medicine for 1 hour three times a week. In older patients, it reduced the progression of dementia and Alzheimer's by 50%. Those with a high risk of diabetes reduced its progression to 58% especially when coupled with other lifestyle changes. Postmenopausal women who used this medicine 4 hours a week reduced their occurrence of hip fractures by 41%. Anxiety was decreased by 48%, and depression by 30% with low doses. When the dose was increased, however, that percentage increased to 47%. Following over 10,000 Harvard alumni over a 12-year period, it was discovered that there was a 23% lower risk of death in those who used the treatment as opposed to those who didn't. It is the number one treatment of fatigue and has been shown over and over again to improve the quality of life.

The lack of exercise or low fitness has also been examined. Steven Blair, a professor at Arnold School of Public Health at the University of South Carolina, performed an Aerobic Centre Longitudinal Study that followed over 50,000 men and women over time. He discovered what happens if certain risk factors are taken away, such as turning a smoker into a non smoker or a couch potato into an active person. In his results he found that low fitness was the strongest predictor of death. (americanfitnessindex.org)

General authorities have also spoken on the importance of exercising the body: John A. Widtsow explained, "The condition of the body limits, largely, the expression of the spirit. The spirit speaks through the body and only as the body permits...Hence, if the body is in poor condition from birth, man must strengthen it as the days increase; if it is strong from the beginning, he must make it stronger." President David O. McKay added, "The healthy man who takes care of his physical being, has strength and vitality; his temple is a fit place for his spirit to reside... It is necessary, therefore, to care for our physical bodies, and observe the laws of physical health and happiness." President Ezra Taft Benson also spoke of the importance of physical well-being. "Physical well-being is not only a priceless asset to one's self–it is also a heritage to be passed on. With good health, all the activities of life are greatly enhanced. A clean mind in a healthy body enables one to render far more effective service to others. It helps one provide more vigorous leadership. It gives our every experience in life more zest and more meaning. Robust health is a noble and worthwhile attainment." And from Marion D. Hanks, "I am grateful to understand that my physical body is an eternal, non-evil component of my eternal soul, and that I have, therefore, a duty to honor and respect and care for it, and refrain from knowingly imposing upon it any treatment or substances deleterious to it. While I could not choose nor govern the condition of the body into which I came, I have the responsibility to give it the best care I can, and if I do not I am acting in derogation of a great gift of God" (Conference Report, Oct. 1958, 109).

Medical doctors, psychologists, professors and prophets all testify to the value of exercise and conversely, the injurious effect of idleness. With so much information and testimony of the benefits of a healthy physical body, it would behoove us all to regard it with as much attention as we do our daily study of the scriptures.

8

THE MIND IS A TERRIBLE
THING TO WASTE

J oseph Smith taught the following in April 1843, later recorded in
Doctrine and Covenants 130:18–19: "Whatever principle of intelligence we attain unto in this life, it will rise with us in the resurrec-
tion. And if a person gains more knowledge and intelligence in this life
through his diligence and obedience than another, he will have so much
the advantage in the world to come."

Seek Knowledge

"Since the early days of the Church, leaders have placed a strong
emphasis on education. The Prophet Joseph Smith, in discussing the
purpose of earth life, consistently stressed learning. He said that one
of the fundamental principles of Mormonism is to 'receive truth let it
come from where it may' (WJS, p. 229). A revelation given to Joseph
Smith stated that 'the glory of God is intelligence' (D&C 93:36). Other
revelations further emphasize the importance of both religious and secular learning: 'Teach ye diligently and my grace shall attend you, that
you may be instructed more perfectly...in all things that pertain unto
the kingdom of God, that are expedient for you to understand; of things

both in heaven and in the earth, and under the earth; things which have been, things which are, things which must shortly come to pass; things which are at home, things which are abroad; the wars and the perplexities of the nations, and the judgments which are on the land; and a knowledge also of countries and of kingdoms' (D&C 88:78-79).

"Brigham Young, the second president of the Church, advanced the same concept, teaching that 'all wisdom, and all the arts and sciences in the world are from God, and are designed for the good of His people' (JD 12:147). These ideas and scriptures have become the foundation of the educational philosophy of the Church (see Education: Attitudes Toward Education).

"As the Saints moved to Ohio, Missouri, and Illinois, they established elementary and secondary schools in each settlement. Schools of the prophets were organized for adult leaders beginning in Kirtland, Ohio, in 1833. In 1840, a university was established in Nauvoo. During their trek to the Rocky Mountains the Saints conducted elementary classes in the temporary camps. In the fall of 1847, just three months after the first company of pioneers arrived in the Salt Lake Valley, schools were organized. Three years following, in 1850, the university of Deseret was founded. (In 1892 the territorial legislature changed the name to the University of Utah.) " Church Educational System (CES)1992 publication.

President David O. McKay said: "True education consists not merely in the acquiring of a few facts of science, history, literature or art, but in the development of character. ...True education trains in self-denial and self-mastery. True education regulates the temper, subdues passion and makes obedience to social laws and moral order a guiding principle of life...

The objective of education is to develop resources in the student that will contribute to his well-being as long as life endures" (*Secrets of a Happy Life*, comp. Llewelyn R. McKay, 1967, 46-47).

President Gordon B. Hinckley wisely counseled the youth of the Church: "The pattern of study you establish during your formal schooling will in large measure affect your lifelong thirst for knowledge. You must get all of the education that you possibly can. ... Sacrifice anything that is needed to be sacrificed to qualify yourselves to do the work of [this] world. ... Train your minds and hands to become an influence for good as you go forward with your lives" ("Seek Learning," *New Era*, Sept. 2007, 2, 4).

President Thomas S. Monson has similarly admonished us, "Beyond our study of spiritual matters, secular learning is also essential...I urge you to pursue your education if you are not already doing so or have not done so–Your talents will expand as you study and learn. You will be able to better assist your families in their learning and you will have peace of mind knowing that you have prepared yourself for the eventualities that you may encounter in life" ("Three Goals to Guide You," *Ensign*, Nov. 2007, 119).

I spent much of my life in educational pursuits. Indeed, it was a family tradition. My father-in-law was a school superintendant, my mother-in-law was an English teacher, my husband was a school principal and I was a school counselor. Several aunts and uncles were teachers. We even had some school bus drivers in the family!

We fostered reading and learning in our home with our children. Spelling words were practiced while other household duties were performed. Parent–teacher conferences were always attended and report cards were scrutinized and discussed.

When our daughter began attending first grade, however, she held a sit-in one morning and refused to go to school. When we questioned her about her decision, she answered emphatically, "I only had to go a half day last year in kindergarten and that worked out just fine! And I already know more than the other kids in the class! So I'm staying home!"

I understood that attending school every day was something that some students found less than desirable. I also knew that students, especially in their teen years, sometimes rebelled against their parents' admonitions to attend school. But I had never encountered such a definitive reaction from such a young child! I was fearful that the next twelve years would indeed seem very long–for both the student and the parents!

In this case, my husband had the calmer head and quickly devised an alternative plan for school. He made a lengthy list of chores and handed the list to our daughter. He then reminded her that her usual job was school, but since she was choosing not to go to school, her job would include all the tasks on the list.

Her eyes grew wide, as did her mouth, and, as if it were humanly possible, she increased the intensity of her voice. "I am not going to do all those chores!" she bellowed. "That will take me forever!"

Her father mentioned that the list would only take six hours, approximately the length of a school day, and she could take a short break for lunch. The rest of the family prepared for the day, leaving this option for her to ponder and no one with whom to argue.

Eventually, and by that I do not mean quickly or quietly, she came to the conclusion that she would go to school. By then, she was late and was in need of an excuse. Her father walked with her to the school, presented her to her teacher, and explained the situation. With a few very convincing "looks" from her father, our daughter was able to wrench out an apology to the teacher for being late for school.

That school year, and the next eleven after that, went as smoothly as is possible for a drama queen. She also continued after high school and attended college, willingly, I might add, and then continued to graduate school. As fate (and pay back) would have it, she later became a teacher–of drama! Perfect!

Seeking knowledge sometimes requires a little convincing from those who are experienced enough to see its value. But the pursuit of knowledge is worth the effort. It doesn't mean you get out of other chores, it just means that you might be able to delegate some of them.

Exercise it!

Elder Robert D. Hales said, "Lifelong learning is essential to the vitality of the human mind, body, and soul. It enhances self-worth and self-actuation. Lifelong learning is invigorating mentally and is a great defense against aging, depression, and self-doubt" ("The Journey of Lifelong Learning," in *Brigham Young University 2008-2009 Speeches*, 8-9).

The words from the prophets regarding the quest for knowledge cannot be disputed. They recognize the value of maintaining a strong mind. One of the best ways to do that is to exercise it. Just as exercise for the body helps to keep it in working order, so does exercising the mind. And keeping both strong will greatly enhance the power of appreciating life even when adversity attacks it.

My father passed away just before his 92nd birthday. In his later years, he had several problems with his physical health, most of which were age related. He walked with the assistance of a walker, had one prosthetic eye, and remote control hearing aids. In spite of this, he still lived in his home, cared for his wife, maintained his financial obligations, and had a perpetual smile. He read the scriptures and the newspaper each day. He had subscriptions to three magazines that he read from cover to cover and had read almost every book in large print in the public library! He is a great example of someone who did his best to maintain a strong mind. In spite of his physical limitations, he still exercised his brain.

While it is important to seek an education, it is also important to be a life long learner. Formal education can be expensive. But, as Derek Bok teaches, "If you think education is expensive, you should try ignorance." Never underestimate, however, the power of reading and working your brain with various activities that do not fall under the umbrella of "formal" education.

I have recently been taking tap and clogging classes. Believe me, I'm not a spring chicken anymore! But I find that the physical strength is just a part of the benefit of the classes. Besides enjoying the company of other women close to my age who are there purely for their own entertainment and a little physical activity, I have recognized the value of the classes to test my brain strength. There are particular steps with specific names that are to be mastered quickly and with some sort of grace and fluidity. I have to keep my legs going in several directions and remember which one to lift, which to kick, which one comes after the other and so on. And it is fast! I've known that exercise is good for mental health, but clogging gave me a new appreciation for "Samanthas" "Cloggovers" and "Fancy Doubles" that were exercising my legs while also exercising my brain!

Doing the crossword puzzles and Sudoku challenges in the newspaper have been a good exercise activity for my brain as well. I now challenge myself on the app on my phone. It's handy while waiting patiently in line at the grocery store or while waiting for the train to cross at the intersection.

Albert Einstein said, "Education is not the learning of facts, but the training of the mind to think." Learning a new skill at any age assists with mental alertness and has been shown in studies to reduce the onset of dementia. It sometimes requires being willing to appear awkward at first, but nothing of value is entirely easy. Memorizing a soliloquy of a Shakespeare play, learning to play a musical instrument, taking a country two-step class with your partner, or learning how to paint are just a few examples. You may even discover more talents while you're at it.

When I was in Primary, we girls learned how to do a cross-stitch sampler. The next year, we learned how to knit and the third year was learning how to crochet. My mother and grandmother assisted me with those skills along with learning how to sew on a sewing machine. I continued those skills in 4-H classes. It was fun to complete a pair of knitted slippers and crochet a purse and even to model a finished dress in the 4-H Fair. But I wasn't totally convinced that I really needed to know any of those skills. I much preferred going outside and running along the ditch bank with the dog or helping my father feed the cows.

My first *real* job interview taught me the lesson that all knowledge gained can be of benefit even when you think, "I'll never need to know this stuff." I had received my bachelor's degree and teaching credentials and had majored in physical education with a minor in English. The junior high school principal with whom I was interviewing was interested in a physical education teacher and coach who could teach a few home economics classes as well–an interesting combination! He asked if I could sew. I answered with a confident *yes*. I had taken a class in high school. I continued to sew my clothes for high school and college but never took college courses in that area. That wasn't his question. I answered honestly.

He asked if I could knit or crochet. I told him I could do both. Again, a truthful answer. He hadn't asked the depth of my skills or inquired about the number of afghans I may or may not have completed. I was hired! I guess you never know when any knowledge you might have gained will be of benefit. I still continue to find knitting, crocheting and sewing valuable skills and appreciate their mind-calming, therapeutic value.

Don't Lose it

Most of us have heard or possibly even shouted the expression: "I am losing my mind!" Most often it comes at a time when a person's to-do list is longer than the Magna Carta and her sleep time equals the temperature at the North Pole. While we can't avoid daily interruptions or unexpected conflicts, we can take measures to care for our mental health with strategies such as time management and problem solving activities.

My husband was the king of Franklin Planners. They included tabs and notes and check marks and lists. It seemed to work well for him. He was definitely organized! He planned everything–business meetings, vacations, finances, shower schedules, and what to wear for the next day, week or season. He color-coded the clothes in his closet and ironed the day before an event. I admire those qualities. I have earnestly endeavored to add some to my daily management style. I have failed.

In an attempt to assist me with my time management, my husband, on one occasion, gave me a Franklin Planner for a gift. It came complete with an invitation to a conference on how to use it. (I was hoping for pearl earrings.) But I valiantly began writing to-do lists in my new organizer. I had arrows for events that were planned forward, check marks for items completed, and an x or two in places that seemed to require them. I tried to choose clothing the night before so I could make sure they were clean and ironed. I carried my planner with me at all times and tried not to lose my colored pencils that separated my work/home/family and church lists. I'm sure the desired result of his thoughtful gift was to create a more organized and productive wife who managed each of the twenty-four hours in her day and didn't stare at the clothes in her closet in the morning chanting, "I have nothing to wear." Instead, the result was a marked spike in my anxiety level. It seemed to take me longer to complete my checks and balances than to do the required tasks. And, I found myself cheating on myself! I would accomplish something I had not written down then cross it off just so I had a checkmark on my list. If I hadn't completed my list by the end of the day, I would have a sense of panic like somehow the Planner Police would barge into my home with dark suits and sunglasses and inspect my work, shake their heads in dismay and put a red "X" on my forehead. Needless to say, that method did not work for me.

I believe in planning. It is essential for putting the important things first and for having an organized life and home, free of clutter–both physically and emotionally. But the *process* of our organization can vary in order to account for a variety of personalities. For me, a big calendar that shows the whole month at once gives me much less anxiety. I can put as many post-it-notes on it as I want, then take them off again and put them in my purse to refer to them later–or in the shredder where no one will know my plans at all. It allows me to accept the unexpected with more patience. I like to call it being spontaneous.

We think of time management as something we have to cram into a 24-hour day. If we don't accomplish our *tasks*, we beat ourselves up, with the result being disappointment and discouragement.

It reminds me of the story of a woman we'll call Susan, who came home one day from taking care of her elderly parent. She was exhausted and had not accomplished the cleaning she had thought she might complete that day. Her perky neighbor met Susan in her driveway and gave her a jar of the jam she had canned. She told Susan how she had picked all the apricots on her tree, and had canned ten quarts of apricots and eight pints of jam. She also had baked bread to go along with it and was now offering her neighbor some of her wares. Susan drew in a deep breath and forced a smile on her face as her neighbor rattled something about service. She squeaked out a shaky, "Thank you," and walked slowly into her house that looked like Hurricane Andrew had stopped by. She peeked out the window of her kitchen to note her back yard that had not been mowed and weeds that had not been pulled. She looked at her neighbor's yard with the perfectly picked apricots and trimmed edges of the green and groomed lawn. She felt that she now had two choices: Quickly close the blinds or move to another neighborhood. She chose the first option–for now.

Had Susan given some perspective to the use of her time that day, she would have realized that the tasks on her to-do list could easily wait for another time, but moments spent with her parent might not. She was giving valuable service and making memories that would last more than one harvest season. Plus, she now had most of the ingredients for a great PB&J!

Organizing our lives and managing our time is definitely a must. It separates urgent activities from non-essential ones. But adding *perspective* allows us to clarify those things and people we value, putting them on the top of our to-do list.

If we take inventory of those things we truly value in our lives, the list becomes very short. Clear away those things you can do without; simplify. You might find a short list that contains something like: 1) I value my relationship with Heavenly Father and Jesus Christ. 2) I value my relationship with family members–on both sides of the veil. 3) I value friendships and desire to nurture them. 4) I value my physical and mental health. 5) I value liberty and justice 6) I value financial peace. Clarifying what we value will allow us to carve out more time in our day on the important goals first. It makes our to-do list more significant. And the huge benefit is less guilt and more peace of mind!

Susan would have had much less guilt about her undone "chores" had she realized that she was strengthening the relationship with her parent, something that was high on her "Things I Value" list. She could also feel less angst toward her perky neighbor, realizing that she valued friendships and was nurturing this one by accepting service cheerfully–also high on her list of values. She could even lie down and take a nap realizing the value of her physical and mental health! By honoring what we value, our goals and lists and daily activities take on much more significance. And we won't feel like we're losing your mind!

Keep it Clean

By gaining knowledge and exercising our minds, we are better able to discern truth from error and contribute to our personal growth. "If your eye be single to [God's] glory, your whole [body and mind] shall be filled with light...and [comprehend] all things" (Doctrine and Covenants 88:67).

Keeping our minds clean has always been an essential part of fulfilling our goal of becoming more Christlike. Yet, it seems that with the wonderful inventions of technology that have been introduced in our time, we have to be more diligent than ever to obtain that goal.

President George Q. Cannon, former counselor in the First Presidency of the Church said: "If a man be pure in thought, he will be correspondingly pure in action; but if he allows his mind to roam in unrestricted freedom in the various avenues of evil or to dwell unchecked upon the contemplation of forbidden indulgences, it will not be long before his feet tread those paths and his hand plucks the tempting but deceitful fruit. When once the tempter gains the citadel of the heart, his power is very great and there is no knowing to what excesses of folly and crime he may incite his unhappy victim." (*Gospel Truth, vol.* 2, Gerald L. Newquist, Salt Lake City: Deseret Book Company, 1974, pg. 200).

"Although there are many wonderful things happening in this day, this is also a time of danger. This is a time to be careful as you have never been careful before. It is a time to be on guard because this is a time 'when men's hearts shall fail them' (Doctrine and Covenants 45:26). This is the time when even the very elect will be deceived... This is a time when Satan is unusually cunning and effective, and he entraps many of us, sometimes without our knowing it.

"When we were born upon the earth, our minds and thoughts were sweet and clean and pure, unpolluted by harmful impurities. In our infancy our minds were free from unwholesome and unrighteous thoughts. We are innocent and untouched by the harmful effects and influences of Satan. Our minds, which are like tremendous reservoirs, are capable of taking in whatever they may be fed, good and bad, righteous thoughts and experiences as well as trash and garbage.

"As we go through life, we may be exposed to stories, pictures, jokes and language or to television shows, videos or movies that are not right for us to see or hear. Our minds will take it all in. They have the capacity to store whatever we give them. Unfortunately, what our minds take in, they keep, sometimes forever.

"It is a long, long process to cleanse a mind that has been polluted by unclean thoughts" (H. Burke Peterson, "Clean Thoughts, Pure Lives," Brigham Young University Devotional, Oct 25, 1983).

The human brain is extraordinarily sensitive to the images it takes in. Thus, pornography which is viewed on the internet or in images in magazines is especially surreptitious and invades the mind in ways that are recently being explained by specialists in the field of psychology.

"Because the human brain is the biological anchor of our psychological experience, it is helpful to understand how it operates," says William

M. Struthers, associate professor of psychology at Wheaton College. "Knowing how it is wired together and where it is sensitive can help us understand why pornography affects people the way it does."

He goes on to explain that sexually explicit material triggers mirror neurons in the brain that correlate to the planning out of behavior. Therefore, "pornography enslaves the viewer to an image, hijacking the biological response intended to bond a man to his wife and therefore loosening that bond."

President Gordon B. Hinckley spoke about pornography in this way: "It grows increasingly worse. It is like a raging storm, destroying individuals and families, utterly ruining what was once wholesome and beautiful." He goes on to describe the statistics that show how pervasive a problem it has become and the toll it takes on a healthy mind.

"I recently read that pornography has become a $57 billion industry worldwide. Twelve billion of this is derived in the United States by evil and "conspiring men" (see D&C 89:4) who seek riches at the expense of the gullible. It is reported that it produces more revenue in the United States than the 'combined revenues of all professional football, baseball and basketball franchises or the combined revenues of ABC, CBS, and NBC'("Internet Pornography Statistics: 2003," Internet, http://www. healthymind.com/5-port-stats.html).

It may be difficult to avoid all contact with pornography on the internet or other readily available visual media. This certainly does not mean we have to embrace it or accept it. Just as we can clean our language, we can clean our thoughts and minds. We can stop putting the garbage in, then clean the receptacle, allowing only pure images and thoughts to enter.

President Hinckley continues, "Suppose a storm is raging and the winds howl and the snow swirls about you. You find yourself unable to stop it. But you can dress properly and seek shelter, and the storm will have no effect upon you.

"Likewise, even though the Internet is saturated with sleazy material, you do not have to watch it. You can retreat to the shelter of the gospel and its teaching of cleanliness and virtue and purity of life ("A Tragic Evil Among Us," *Ensign*, Nov. 2004, 61).

"All of imagination–everything that we think, we feel, we sense–comes through the human brain. And once we create new patterns in this brain, once we shape the brain in a new way, it never returns to its original shape" (Jay S. Walker, www.brainyquote.com).

May we "shape our brain" with pure thoughts, wonderful words and worthwhile images.

9

Take Care of Your Soul

I'm not yet certain of the exact definition of "soul." It lies somewhere close to the spirit. Perhaps, the words "soul" and "spirit" could be interchangeable. But I like to consider the soul as that part of a body that makes us human. Again, that could be the definition of our spirit. But for my purposes, I would like to define the soul as those God-given talents and characteristics that make us who we are as individuals. No one is exactly the same. We all have strengths and weaknesses. We all have those things about which we are passionate, those things that thrill us and interest us, while another would find those same experiences dull and boring endeavors, unworthy of their time and attention.

I see the soul as a bit of a separate but unified part of the human experience. The spirit assures we are alive. The soul assures we are living. Really living. So how do we nurture our souls?

Celebrate Your Individuality

In Robert Fulghum's book, *All I Really Need to Know I Learned in Kindergarten,* he describes a situation in which he was left in charge of about eighty children seven to ten years old at a church social hall while their parents were off doing "parenty" things. He devised a game which he called, Giants, Wizards and Dwarfs. It was a large-scale version of Rock, Paper, and Scissors and involved a lot of noise and running around. While they whirled about, he yelled, "You have to decide now which you are–a giant, a wizard or a dwarf!"

While the groups huddled in frenzied, whispered consultation, one small child tugged at his pants leg and asked, "Where do the Mermaids stand?"

After a long pause, he finally told her there were no such things as Mermaids. She disagreed with him replying, "Yes there are! I am one!"

He describes the situation this way: "She did not relate to being a Giant, a Wizard or a Dwarf. She knew her category, Mermaid. And she was not about to leave the game and go over and stand against the wall where a loser would stand. She intended to participate, wherever Mermaids fit into the scheme of things. Without giving up dignity or identity. She took it for granted that there was a place for Mermaids and that I would know just where.

"Well, where DO the Mermaids stand? All the "Mermaids"–all those who are different, who do not fit the norm and who do not accept the available boxes and pigeonholes? Answer that question and you can build a school, a nation, or a world on it."

He cleverly replied that the Mermaids were to stand right next to him because he was the King of the Sea. And it gave him great pleasure to realize that mermaids did indeed exist. He got to meet one personally. (81-83)

I love the spunk and self-confidence of this little child. I hope her individuality is never squashed by someone attempting to place her brightly colored package into a slot meant for letters only.

Elder Dieter F. Uchtdorf, spoke at a Church Educational Fireside and shared the story of the Ugly Duckling with the youth who attended. He expressed to them that, like the Hans Christian Anderson story, it was important to become aware of who they really are.

"In reality, said Elder Uchtdorf, we are elegant and eternal creatures of infinite value with potential beyond imagination. Discovering who we really are is part of this great adventure called life."

He continued, "It is my earnest prayer that the knowledge of who you are and what you may become will fill your souls with the peaceable love of God and that this will ignite within you a happiness worthy of your true heritage, for in truth you are princes and princesses, kings and queens " ("The Reflection in the Water", CES Devotional, 2009).

Often times we find it difficult to be grateful for ourselves. Most often this happens as a result of comparing our worst faults with someone else's greatest assets. But observe the beauty of a quilt with its many patterns. There is variety in size and shape, color, texture and print. That is what makes it beautiful. The same is true with us.

I recently sat in church next to an adorable young woman. I had not met her before and it was pleasant getting acquainted. She was cheerful, had a lovely smile and her comments were thought-provoking. As our conversation continued, she happened to cross her legs. It was difficult not to notice how long, shapely, tan and flawless they were! I immediately pulled my skirt a little farther over my short, stubby, white legs with veins that resemble the Los Angeles Freeway System. It wasn't that I was coveting her legs. (Well, maybe a little bit.) But I was certainly comparing hers to mine—and in my mind, I didn't measure up! I have been blessed with some very fine qualities. But at that moment, I couldn't think of any. And as my age progresses, those qualities are definitely more inward than outward! I tend to forget that for all their cosmetic faults, my legs work just fine. They carry me where I want to go. They have taken me down snow-filled, alpine slopes and up majestic hiking trails. They have been strong as I have carried children and they never fail me as I shop the malls. I have two of them. They reach the ground and I can move them around. Perspective is an important and needful quality when it comes to recognizing our importance.

Appearances are not the only thing we tend to compare. We often look to others and their remarkable accomplishments that have been heroic, or at the very least, noted in the newspaper. We compare that to our seemingly unremarkable lives, and wonder about our very value.

One example is from a favorite Christmas movie of mine, starring Jimmy Stewart. *It's a Wonderful Life*, is the story of George Baily who resides in the small town of Bedford Falls. He lives there with his wife and children and manages a family-owned building and loan company. He has had dreams and ambitions. Perhaps he would build wonderful skyscrapers or travel the world. Instead, he chose to sacrifice those ambitions for his brother and the people in his town.

When, on Christmas Eve, George's uncle loses $8,000 that was to be deposited, George feels the weight of the town–and the world–on his shoulders. He has felt that his life has been insignificant, but this is a defining moment for George. He feels responsible for the loss, the probable collapse of his company and the foreseeable prospect of Mr. Potter taking over the town. He feels that his wife and children, and indeed the whole town, would be better off if he didn't exist.

As he contemplates taking his life by jumping off a bridge, he is saved by Clarence, an angel who earns his wings by showing George the miserable state of his family and the town had he not been a part of their lives. He had only been kind to people and dealt fairly with them. He raised a loving family and cared for his wife. Because of his disappointments, he could not see the powerful impact those seemingly insignificant deeds had on the lives of many. In the end, he is brought back to the reality that his friends and family love him and have prayed for him. They then return his kindnesses by rallying behind him and raising the needed money to keep the business open.

Many people are like George. They live their lives in quiet service. They raise families and teach them to work hard and be honest. They never make the front page of the newspaper or win "important" awards. They may even think their lives have been dull and inconsequential. But to those of us who have benefitted from parents who simply loved us, provided for our needs and taught us to work hard and pray often, it is anything BUT insignificant. Neither of my parents attended college, but I was indeed instructed well because of their tutelage. Neither of them won trophies, built tall buildings or became famous. But they did plant crops, served their country, raised good kids and were examples of honesty, integrity and cheerful service in their community and church. And the ripple effect of their lives will last much longer and flow much further than an award placed in a trophy case.

The teacher who believes in his students' abilities when few others do, the father who spends his Saturday helping his child learn to ride a bike, the mother who spends more time carrying on a conversation with her toddler than talking to her friends, the neighbor who cares for the elderly couple living across the street—these are all noble acts. They may seem small and simple, but ..."by small and simple things are great things brought to pass..." (Alma 37:6).

"I believe in myself," said President Gordon B. Hinckley. "I do not mean to say this with egotism. But I believe in my capacity and in your capacity to do good, to make some contribution to the society of which we are a part, to grow and develop, and to do things that we may now think impossible.

"I believe I am a child of God, endowed with a divine birthright. I believe that there is something of divinity within me and within each of you. I believe that we have a godly inheritance and that it is our responsibility, our obligation, and our opportunity to cultivate and nurture the very best of these qualities within us" ("I Believe," *Ensign,* Aug. 1992).

As Helen Keller observed, "I long to accomplish great and noble tasks, but it is my chief duty to accomplish humble tasks as though they were great and noble. The world is moved along, not only by the mighty shoves of its heroes, but also by the aggregate of the tiny pushes of each honest worker."

Celebrate the Wonders of Life

A group of geography students studied the Seven Wonders of the World. At the end of that section, the students were asked to list what they considered to be those wonders. Though there was some disagreement, the following got the most votes: Egypt's Great Pyramids, Taj Mahal, Grand Canyon, Panama Canal, Empire State Building, St. Peter's Basilica and China's Great Wall. While gathering the votes, the teacher noted that one student, a quiet girl, hadn't turned in her paper yet. So she asked the girl if she was having trouble with her list. The girl replied, "yes, a little. I couldn't quite make up my mind because there were so many." The teacher said, "Well, tell us what you have and maybe we can help." The girl hesitated, then read, "I think the Seven Wonders of the World are: to touch, to taste, to see, to hear." She hesitated a little, then "To run, to laugh and to love."

I love this example because it teaches us that we may be assisted in our pursuit of joy by seeing life through the eyes of a child who recognizes the wonders of God. Sometimes as adults, in our efforts to do our jobs and complete daily chores, we miss out on some daily pleasures. There is wonder in each day. We don't have to be practical *all* the time. Although each person seeks joy differently, and those pursuits change with the seasons of our lives, it is important to seek joy in our daily journey. While it is good to avoid immediate gratification, it wouldn't hurt to take advantage of those small pleasures before they quickly flee away.

I grew up in a very humble home surrounded by fields and a dairy barn. It was not often that new furniture came into the house. Any extra money was usually used first for more *needful* things, such as a new plow or a new cow. I recall that my mother left the plastic on our new turquoise blue couch for at least a year. We also used melmac dishes every day, while the "good" ones received as a wedding gift were left in the cedar chest along with the crocheted tablecloth. It is understandable for those who sacrificed during the Great Depression to be vigilant about protecting their cherished items. That type of practicality was deeply ingrained in me as well. Later, however, a few significant moments caused me to change my thinking and some of my habits.

My mother suddenly passed away from a blood clot at the age of fifty-six. It was unexpected and untimely. I was grief stricken–for myself and for my father. I knew that my parents had waited patiently until the time they could retire and go on a vacation–maybe a cruise. They had just sold the farm and were starting to enjoy a new season of life. They had worked so hard and sacrificed so much and now wouldn't be able to enjoy this time together. This caused me even more heartache.

Three months after my mother's passing, I read an article in a Woman's Day Magazine that had a powerful impact upon me. It was about a woman who had just helped her friend go through her late mother-in-law's possessions–deciding what to sell, what to keep and what to give to charity. "On the rack in the kitchen were tattered tea towels. But in the linen closet was a lifetime supply of beautifully embroidered towels that had never been used. The nightie that lay across the foot of the bed was faded and shapeless, though a stack of never-worn gowns was carefully stored in the bureau drawer, some still in their original boxes. And so it went throughout the house." She went on to illustrate how she herself habitually wore some drab, ugly clothes–even when she wasn't cleaning the oven–in order to "save" the attractive outfits she really liked. She wasn't suggesting we all go crazy and ditch our responsibilities, spend every penny of our savings and go on a self-indulgent journey while kicking our fellow man to the curb. But she did recognize that our tendency to overestimate the importance of tasks often prevents us from enjoying life's small delights and big adventures. She continued, "I want to change more than my attitude toward possessions, for practicality can also lead to self-denial of the spirit. Getting the dinner dishes done becomes more important than enjoying the magic of a sunset. Finishing the mending ranks higher on the priority list than reading the children a second bedtime story.

"So I am going to change. Not drastically–just by making a few adjustments. Special occasions will be redefined to include not only Christmas and Easter, but when we've finished the income taxes ahead of schedule or the cat has gone six months without seeing the vet. Days with beautiful skies and melting snow will also qualify for celebration. And whenever I'm faced with alternate choices, I plan to weigh their practicality on a somewhat different scale than I've used in the past. (Connie Emerson, "Farewell to Sunday-Best," *Woman's Day*, Mar. 1984).

Some of my greatest memories are the times when I've put down my to-do list and involved myself in the joy of the moment. When our children were younger, they enjoyed playing with the other neighborhood children. More often than not, their activities took place in our home or yard. At the time, I wondered why I had to be the "appointed" one to supervise. But I revel in the memories I now have of the days I took time to "play." Hopefully, our children also remember making swords and armor out of tin foil, or going on bicycles to the "dirt hills," flying kites, running through the sprinkler, having backyard badminton contests, catching their first fish, or sitting around a campfire laughing, telling stories and roasting marshmallows.

And then there were the fashion shows when several girls gathered in our daughter's room to dress up. I was enlisted to be the narrator of the fashion show by sitting on a stool at the bottom of the stairs and describing the beautiful, gorgeous, divine "lady" as she pranced proudly down the stairs in her gown. None continued on to become Miss America. But hopefully, they remember the day that, for a while, they were the queen of the universe.

"In all living have much of fun and laughter. Life is to be enjoyed, not just endured." (President Gordon B. Hinckley)

Listen to Your Soul

I believe that if we take the time to evaluate ourselves, we will recognize a dream or yearning inside that is bursting to come forth. These dreams may take form at different seasons of our lives or may have been inside us since we can remember and are a part of us still. You may be living your dream right now–or at least working toward it. I think it is the reason for choosing a particular vocation; it is certainly the purpose for our hobbies. It satisfies our desires, it magnifies our talents, it adds pep to our step and it brings joy to our souls.

In her book, *The Gifts of Imperfection*, Brene' Brown researched the idea of "meaningful work" in connection to living a "wholehearted" life. "This is what emerged: *We all have gifts and talents.* When we cultivate those gifts and share them with the world, we create a sense of meaning and purpose in our lives. *Squandering our gifts brings distress to our lives.* It's not merely benign or "too bad" if we don't use the gifts that we've been given; we pay for it with our emotional and physical well-being. *Sharing our gifts and talents with the world is the most powerful source of connection with God.* *Using our gifts and talents to create meaningful work takes a tremendous amount of commitment.* In many cases, the meaningful work is not what pays the bills... they use their gifts and talents to do work that feeds their souls... *Like our gifts and talents, meaning is unique to each of us*" (112).

Finding the activities that bring personal enjoyment, certainly adds a spark to every-day living. But what if we never ignite enough sparks to start a fire? What if we never fulfill–or even explore–that thing about which we feel passion?

I am an admirer of poets who can create a vast amount of sentiment using very few words. Here are two "Dream" poems that have given me much food for thought:

Dream Deferred
By Langston Hughes

What happens to a dream deferred?
Does it dry up
like a raisin in the sun?
Or fester like a sore–
And then run?
Does it stink like rotten meat?
Or crust and sugar over–

129

like a syrupy sweet?
Maybe it just sags
like a heavy load.
Or does it explode?

In this poem, Hughes is presenting us with a question. What happens if a dream is deferred? Does it sag, explode, or fester? The answer to that question lies within each individual. Perhaps this prompts other questions, however: What happens if you never work toward fulfilling a dream? Can you identify your dreams? Do you know what feeds your soul? What happens when your soul is starving? Are dreams and goals the same? How much are you willing to sacrifice? For what? For whom? Can dreams be replaced, renewed, revised? Again, the answers lie within us. Our task is to listen to our souls and work to satisfy its yearning.

In this poem by Robert Frost, we are given some light-hearted but sagely advice concerning the matter:

In a Glass of Cider

It seemed I was a mite of sediment
That waited for the bottom to ferment
So I could catch a bubble in ascent.
I rode up on one till the bubble burst
And when that left me to sink back reversed
I was no worse off than I was at first.
I'd catch another if I waited.
The thing was to get now and then elated.

Frost is expressing his belief that our lives are buoyed up by taking chances, maybe even a risk or two. He asserts that not all hopes and dreams will end in the desired result. We may end up back where we started. With patience and time, however, we can grasp another opportunity and see where that takes us. The idea is to go for it! Grab that "bubble" and hold on! Don't sit idle.

We have each been given gifts and talents. The parable of the talents gives added insight into the value of using those resources. In Matthew 25:14-30, we read of a man who offers his servants of his goods. "And unto one he gave five talents, to another two, and to another one; to every man according to his several ability...Then he that had received the five talents went and traded with the same, and made them other five talents. And likewise he that had received two, he also gained other two. But he that had received one went and digged the earth, and hid his lord's money."

Later, the lord came back and asked his servants to give an accounting of how their talents were used. The one with five talents had gained five more. The servant with two talents had doubled his as well. But the servant with one talent confessed that he had been afraid and had hid his talent in the earth. The lord praised the first two servants and remarked, "thou hast been faithful over a few things, I will make thee ruler over many things: enter thou into the joy of thy lord." But the servant who had buried his talent, was told he had been slothful and would therefore be cast out.

This simple story teaches a powerful truth. Whatever gifts, blessings or talents we are given in this life are to be shared, used and made better through their use. It would behoove each of us to listen to our souls so we can recognize our talents and how best to share them and improve upon them.

"The desire to create is one of the deepest yearnings of the human soul. No matter our talents, education, backgrounds, or abilities, we each have an inherent wish to create something that did not exist before... The bounds of creativity extend far beyond the limits of a canvas or a sheet of paper and do not require a brush, a pen, or the keys of a piano. As you take the normal opportunities of your daily life and create something of beauty and helpfulness, you improve not only the world around you but also the world within you" (Dieter F. Uchtdorf, "Happiness, Your Heritage," *General Relief Society Broadcast,* Oct. 2008).

10

SHINE ON WITH THE SPIRIT

The soul and the spirit are alluded to many times in the scriptures. I like this definition which contrasts the two of them: "The soul is the essence of humanity's being; it is who we are. The spirit is the aspect of humanity that connects with God." (Got question.org)

It is readily accepted by the world that without our spirit, our bodies are basically a shell. The spirit is what makes us a living entity. What might not be so readily accepted is the fact that our spirits allow us the opportunity to communicate with God. "It must...be understood that the Holy Ghost is the medium through whom God and his Son, Jesus Christ, communicate with men [and women] upon the earth" (*A Marvelous Work and a Wonder*, Legrand Richards, pg. 119).

If we are indeed spiritual beings, and we are, our spirits become enlightened through the Spirit of God or Light of Christ. "But there is a spirit in man; and the inspiration of the Almighty giveth them understanding" (Job 32:8). Some refer to this enlightenment as a sixth sense, an "Aha" moment, a gut feeling or a conscience. It is indeed the Holy Ghost.

When Jesus spoke to his apostles in the Garden of Gethsemane, he said, "I will not leave you comfortless... But the Comforter, which is the Holy Ghost, whom the Father will send in my name, he shall teach you all things and bring all things to your remembrance, whatsoever I have said unto you" (John 14:18, 26).

The Gift of the Holy Ghost

The gift of the Holy Ghost is somewhat different from the Spirit of God. While all of us receive the Spirit of God, the power of the Gift of the Holy Ghost is received only after one is baptized. It is received by the laying on of hands by those who have the priesthood authority to bestow that gift. Elder James E. Faust described the difference by observing, "Those possessing the gift of the Holy Ghost can come to a greater light and testimony. The Holy Ghost bears witness of the truth and impresses upon the soul the reality of God the Father and the Son Jesus Christ so deeply that no earthly power or authority can separate him from that knowledge" ("The Gift of the Holy Ghost–A Sure Compass," *Ensign*, Apr. 1996).

"And then are ye in this strait and narrow path which leads to eternal life; yea, ye have entered in by the gate; ye have done according to the commandments of the Father and the Son; and ye have received the Holy Ghost, which witnesses of the Father and the Son, unto the fulfilling of the promise which he hath made, that if ye entered in by the way ye should receive" (2 Nephi 31:18).

Elder Larry Lawrence put it this way while contrasting the Light of Christ with the gift of the Holy Ghost, "Without the gift of the Holy Ghost, we are like a person walking slowly home in the dark with only a flashlight as a guide. When we accept the gospel of Jesus Christ and are baptized, we are offered a floodlight and a guide who knows the way. Now we can walk faster and see our way during our homeward journey" ("The Light of the Perfect Day," *Ensign*, March 2016).

The Holy Ghost is a member of the Godhead. Unlike Heavenly Father and Jesus Christ, he is a personage of spirit. That allows our spirit to "feel" the spirit of the Holy Ghost. "The Father has a body of flesh and bones as tangible as man's; the Son also; but the Holy Ghost has not a body of flesh and bones, but is a personage of Spirit. Were it not so, the Holy Ghost could not dwell in us" (D&C 130:22).

A Spirit of Peace and Happiness

Perhaps as important as understanding the characteristics of the Holy Ghost, is recognizing how important it is to our entire well-being. I love this explanation by President James E. Faust, "I believe the Spirit of the Holy Ghost is the greatest guarantor of inward peace in our unstable world. It can be more mind-expanding and can make us have a better sense of well-being than any chemical or other earthly substance. It will calm nerves; it will breathe peace to our souls. This Comforter can be with us as we seek to improve. It can function as a source of revelation to warn us of impending danger and also help keep us from making mistakes. It can enhance our natural senses so that we can see more clearly, hear more keenly, and remember what we should remember. It is a way of maximizing our happiness" ("The Gift of the Holy Ghost–A Sure Compass," *Ensign,* Apr. 1996).

Brigham Young tells of an experience when in a dream or vision, the prophet Joseph Smith appeared to him. He asked the Prophet what message he should take to people of the Church. The Prophet told him to "Tell the people to be humble and faithful, and be sure to keep the spirit of the Lord and it will lead them right... [The spirit] will whisper peace and joy to their souls; it will take malice, hatred, strife and all evil from their hearts; and their whole desire will be to do good, bring forth righteousness and build up the kingdom of God" (*Manuscript History of Brigham Young,* 1846-1847, comp. Elden J. Watson, Salt Lake City, 1971, p. 529).

Jesus Christ is often called the Prince of Peace. "We know not what lies ahead of us," said President Gordon B. Hinckley. "We know not what the coming days will bring. We live in a world of uncertainty. For some, there will be great accomplishment. For others, disappointment. For some, much of rejoicing and gladness, good health, and gracious living. For others, perhaps sickness and a measure of sorrow. We do not know. But one thing we do know. Like the polar star in the heavens, regardless of what the future holds, there stands the Redeemer of the world, the Son of God, certain and sure as the anchor of our immortal lives. He is the rock of our salvation, our strength, our comfort, the very focus of our faith" (*Teachings of the Presidents of the Church*, pg.137). The Holy Ghost can testify to us of this truth and help provide that comfort to our souls. Who wouldn't want to feel comfort, strength and inward peace? Who wouldn't want to maximize their happiness?

The Holy Ghost as a Guide

We have many opportunities to receive guidance in our lives. Parents and teachers give us instruction. The scriptures provide insight and direction. The guidance of our modern prophets offer more truths and standards to enrich our understanding. In addition, the Holy Ghost can be our personal compass. And it is up to each of us to discover how that compass operates as a guiding and protective influence in our lives.

Julie B. Beck, former General Relief Society President, said this about its guiding influence, "The ability to qualify for, receive, and act on personal revelation is the single most important ability that can be acquired in this life...Education is wonderful, but being able to feel the Lord's power and Spirit upon us is the highest education we can achieve. With that, we have power and influence. Without it, we will not be able to navigate in this life. The adversary will pick us off one by one, and we will be drawn off course by the many, many voices that are out there distracting us. With the Lord's Spirit upon us, we are strong and solid and will be able to walk with Him" (BYU Women's Conference, April 29, 2010).

It is easy to recognize the blaring sound of a smoke alarm. It warns us of impending danger, giving us the sure message that we should act. Promptly! The voice of the spirit is not as easily recognized. It requires practice and prayer to decipher the warnings, suggestions, feelings and whisperings. And it seems to enlighten our spirit in just the personal manner that will be most helpful to each individual.

President Gordon B. Hinckley tells of a time when he was giving counsel to new mission presidents. He told of instruction he received from President Harold B. Lee when he was being set apart as a stake president.

"I remember only one thing he said: 'Listen for the whisperings of the Spirit in the middle of the night, and respond to those whisperings.' I don't know why revelation comes sometimes in the night but it does. It comes in the day as well, of course. But listen to the whisperings of the Spirit, the gift of revelation, to which you are entitled" (*Teachings of the Presidents of the Church: Gordon B. Hinckley*, 2016, 556).

He continued to recall for them an experience he had when he was in Hong Kong with other church leaders as they searched for a place to build a temple. He went to bed feeling unsettled about the decision he had to make, but was awakened early the next morning with some enlightening thoughts.

"Something very interesting came to my mind," he recorded in his journal. "I did not hear a voice with my natural ears. But to my mind there came the voice of the Spirit. It said, 'Why are you worried about this? You have a wonderful piece of property where the mission home and the small chapel stand...Build a building of [several] stories. It can include a chapel and classrooms on the first two floors and a temple on the top of two or three floors.' Having received that revelation, President Hinckley said, "I relaxed and went back to sleep" (Sheri L. Dew, *Go Forward With Faith: The Biography of Gordon B. Hinckley* 1996, 481).

That same type of revelation can come to each of us for our individual concerns. We can have feelings of calm as opposed to unsettled feelings. We can hear promptings that are unlike voices heard with our natural ears. And those whisperings often come when our mind is not busy with the loud interrupting voices of the world around us.

For me, the spirit seems to prompt with a feeling more often than a whispering. And sometimes thoughts enter into my mind that I have since recognized came after much searching, pondering and praying. Sometimes, I have resisted those prompting thoughts, and discovered later my folly. It is becoming easier to recognize when I feel the spirit of love, truth and calm, or when I am feeling and hearing the voice of warning.

On one occasion, shortly before graduating from high school I had, what I describe, as a vivid "Come to Jesus Meeting" with the Holy Ghost. I had decided that after graduation, I would enter a training course for airline stewardesses where I would fly the friendly skies and travel the world in style. I had only traveled outside the state of Idaho on three occasions and that was with my family in our trusty used car and usually to a relative's house or a National Park. I had never flown on a plane, and I seldom left the sight of the small farming community in which I lived. That did not deter me. I was excited about the prospect of getting off the farm and figured this was my opportunity. I pictured myself in my stewardess uniform, walking through airports as young children stared in admiration –much like the movie, *Catch Me if You Can* starring Leonardo DiCaprio. It would be exhilarating, invigorating, thrilling! I talked my parents into the idea. They were noticeably skeptical, but attempted to be supportive. They even paid a small down payment to the representative who came to our home to discuss the details. This was just the glorious future I was hoping for.

Apparently, God had other plans. A few weeks later, I began having uneasy feelings about my decision. I had not asked the Lord beforehand if He thought this was a good idea, but figured He would certainly know how enthusiastic I was about my intentions. I dismissed the feelings as the "jitters" about starting something new. The uneasy feelings started to increase into feelings of dread. I still resisted. Surely, Heavenly Father knew how much I wanted adventure! Surely, He knew how adorable I would look in my uniform and how proud I would be at my class reunion to tell my classmates about all the exotic lands I had traveled. The feelings of dread started making me feel physically ill. I knew where the feelings were coming from but I was too proud to admit it. I knew these were promptings and warnings from God, via the Holy Ghost. Still reluctant, but finally admitting defeat, I said, "Fine! I'll go to college for a year. But THEN I'm going to be a stewardess." I'm not sure whom I was talking to, but it was as if I needed to shout back to the voice that seemed to be shouting at me. Maybe hardheaded people need a little more than whisperings to penetrate their skulls.

I went humbly to my parents to tell them my new plan. I apologized for the money they had paid, knowing how little they had and that they wouldn't get all of it back. They didn't seem to be upset! They didn't lecture me about changing my mind or discourage me from applying to college. Could it be that their prayers had been answered? Funny how that works.

I did indeed go to college. I had no jitters. I embraced learning and new relationships. I never left school to become a stewardess. Instead, I married a wonderful young man, actually my high school sweetheart, and together we completed college and received our degrees. Together, we have been able to travel many times to many places being served by many airline hostesses. And somehow, I don't envy them at all.

I have since realized how instrumental that one decision has been in my life. I could very easily have gone not just close to the edge of the straight and narrow path, but jumped right over the fence and sprinted so far into the horizon I would never have found my way back. Also, I have come to recognize how significant it has been to my future endeavors to have gone to college and earned a degree. Now, I am much less resistant to the promptings of the Spirit and feel blessed each day to have that Spirit with me as my guide and compass.

Inviting the Spirit

As we partake of the sacrament, we have an opportunity to reflect, in a reverent atmosphere, about our Savior, Jesus Christ. The last phrases of the sacrament prayer are: "that they do always remember Him, that they may have his Spirit to be with them" (D&C 20:77,79). We should not think that by partaking of the sacrament alone, we will always have the Spirit to be with us. Indeed, the Holy Ghost can abide with us wherever we go or whatever we do *as long as where we go and what we do are places he will dwell,* for "the Spirit of the Lord doth not dwell in unholy temples" (Helaman 4:24).

"We should endeavor to discern when we 'withdraw [ourselves] from the Spirit of the Lord, that it may have no place in [us] to guide [us] in wisdom's paths that we may be blessed, prospered, and pre-served' (Mosiah 2:36). Precisely because the promised blessing is *that we may always have His Spirit to be with us,* we should attend to and learn from the choices and influences that separate us from the Holy Spirit.

"The standard is clear. If something we think, see, hear, or do dis-tances us from the Holy Ghost, then we should stop thinking, seeing, hearing, or doing that thing. If that which is intended to entertain, for example, alienates us from the Holy Spirit, then certainly that type of entertainment is not for us. Because the Spirit cannot abide that which is vulgar, crude, or immodest, then clearly such things are not for us. Because we estrange the Spirit of the Lord when we engage in activities we know we should shun, then such things definitely are not for us" (Elder David A. Bednar, "That We May Always Have His Spirit to Be with Us," *Ensign*, May 2006).

We invite the Spirit by keeping the commandments of God. If that seems overwhelming, then we can work on one small aspect of the Gospel at a time. The wonderful thing about the Spirit is that it is customized for each one of us. He tells us what we need to hear at the time. "The Holy ghost doesn't tell us to improve everything at once. If He did, we would become discouraged and give up. The Spirit works with us at our own speed, one step at a time"... (Elder Larry R. Lawrence, "What Lack I Yet?" October General Conference, 2015).

Elder Lawrence gave an example of how we can invite the Spirit in order to receive personal inspiration. He told of a faithful mother who humbled herself and asked the Lord what was keeping her from progressing. "In her case, the response from the Spirit came immediately: 'Stop complaining.' This answer surprised her; she had never thought of herself as a complainer. However, the message from the Holy Ghost was very clear. In the days that followed, she became conscious of her habit of complaining. Grateful for the prompting to improve, she determined to count her blessings instead of her challenges. Within days, she felt the warm approval of the Spirit."

President Harold B. Lee taught, "Every one of us, if we reach perfection, must [at] one time ask ourselves this question, 'What lack I yet?'" (*Teachings of the Presidents of the Church: Harold B. Lee* (2000), pg.197). This is key to inviting the Spirit. We need to humble ourselves, and ask the Lord in prayer what we can do to improve our lives in order to find more peace and happiness. With each answer and each improvement, we can find the joy that we seek.

Elder Richard G. Scott: "You are unavoidably immersed in a sea of persistent, worldly pressures that could destroy your happiness, if you let them. Yet these very forces, squarely faced, provide opportunity for tremendous personal growth and development. When you conquer adversity, it produces strength of character, forges self-confidence, engenders self-respect, and assures success in righteous endeavor. When you master growth challenges, you are rewarded with satisfying happiness. Through that means you will confirm that life can be lived on a continuing foundation of happiness."

And so...

If we humble ourselves and sincerely ask the Lord how we can find more joy, more peace and more contentment, He will answer with whisperings to our hearts. We might get the impression to work less at appearing to be perfect, and work harder at perfecting ourselves. We may receive the impression to forgive someone or serve someone. We might feel impressed to stop envying or harboring guilt. Maybe it will be to get up and walk for thirty minutes or fuel our body with more nutritious foods or take time to play a game with our children.

The idea is to rid ourselves of whatever is keeping us from finding happiness. Then keep growing and praying and improving so when life's lumps come our way, we can still find joy–no matter the circumstances. And so... go get a kick out of life!

SOURCES CITED

Aristotle. "Metaphysics of Morals." *Rhetoric.* 4th Century B.C.

Ashton, Marvin J. "On Being Worthy." *Ensign*, May 1989, 20.

Baumeister, R.F. & Leary, M. R. " The Need to Belong: Desire for Interpersonal Attachments as a Fundamental Human Motivation." *Psychological Bulletin,* 117.

Beck, Julie B. "Choose Ye This Day to Serve the Lord." BYU Women's Conference, April, 2010.

Bednar, David A. "And Nothing Shall Offend Them." *Liahona*, November 2006, 89.

Benson, Ezra Taft. "Beware of Pride." *Ensign,* May 1984, 4.

_____. "The Faces of Pride." *New Era*, October 2003, 40.

_____. "To Increase in the Wisdom and Favor with God and Man." *New Era*, September 1979.

Book of Mormon Video Presentations. "Becoming Children of Christ." Salt lake City: The Church of Jesus Christ of Latter Day Saints.

Blair, Dr. Steven N. "Aerobic Centre Longitudinal Study." University of South Carolina. 2008.

Brown, Brene'. *The Gifts of Imperfection.* Center City, Minnesota: Hazelden Publishing, 2010.

Burton, H. David. "Courage to Hearken." *Ensign,* May 1994, 66.

Capra, Frank, producer. *It's a Wonderful Life.* California: Liberty Films, 1946.

Carlin, John. *Playing the Enemy.* London: Atlantic Books, 2008.

CDC.gov/std/stats 10.

Church Educational System (CES) Salt Lake City: The Church of Jesus Christ of Latter-day Saints, 1992.

Dew, Sheri. *Go Forward With Faith: The Biography of Gordon B. Hinckley.* Salt Lake City: Deseret Book, 1996.

_____. *No One Can Take Your Place.* Salt Lake City: Deseret Book, 2004.

Emerson, Connie. "Farewell to Sunday-Best." *Woman's Day,* March 1984.

Evans, Dr. Michael. *23 ½ Hours,* University of Toronto, 2010.

"The Family: A Proclamation to the World." Salt Lake City: The Church of Jesus Christ of Latter-day Saints, 1995.

Faust, James E. "The Gift of the Holy Ghost–A Sure Compass." *Ensign,* April 1996.

Fulghum, Robert. *All I Really Need to Know I Learned in Kindergarten,* New York City: Ballantine Publishing Group, 1986.

Grant, Heber J. "Hyrum and His Distinguished Posterity." *Improvement Era,* August, 1998, 54-55.

Goaslind, Jack H. "Reach Out to Our Father's Children." *Ensign,* May 1981, 59.

Hales, Robert D. "The Journey of Lifelong Learning." *Brigham Young University Speeches,* 2008-2009, 8-9.

Hanks, Marion D. "For Man Is Spirit." *Conference Report,* October 1958, 107-110.

Hinckley, Gordon B. "A Tragic Evil Among Us." *Ensign,* November 2004, 61.

_____. "A Prophet's Counsel and Prayer for Youth." *Ensign,* January 2001.

_____. "An Ensign to the Nations." *Ensign,* November 1989, 52.

_____. "'Of You It Is Required to Forgive.'" *Ensign,* November 1980, 61.

_____. "Seek Learning." *New Era,* September 2007, 2, 4.

_____. "The Scourge of Illicit Drugs." *Ensign,* November 1989, 48.

_____. "Thou Shalt Not Covet." *Ensign,* March 1990, 2.

_____. "Words of the Prophet: You Can Be Forgiven." *New Era,* October 2001, 4.

Holland, Jeffrey R. "The Other Prodigal." *Liahona,* July 2002, 69-72.

http://en.wikipedia.org/Amish school shooting.

Hurst, James. "The Scarlet Ibis." *The Atlantic Monthly,* 1960.

Jensen, Marlin K. "To Walk Humbly with Thy God." *Liahona,* July 2001, 11.

Jones, Jenkin Lloyd, "Who Is Tampering with the Soul of America?" Speech first delivered to Inland Daily Press Association, Chicago, 1962.

Journal of Discourses, London: Latter-day Saints Book Depot, 1854-1886.

Kimball, Spencer W. "The Davids and the Goliaths." *Ensign,* November 1974, 80.

Lawrence, Larry. "The Light of the Perfect Day." *Ensign*, March 2016, 64.

_____. "What Lack I Yet?" Ensign. October 2015, 33.

Lewis, C.S. *Mere Christianity*. New York: Macmillan, 1952.

_____. *The Screwtape Letters*, New York: Touchstone, 1996.

LDS.org–Topic Definition–"Plan of Salvation."

Mandino, Og. *A Better Way to Live*. New York City: Bantam Books, 1990.

Mason, James O. "I Have a Question." Ensign, September 1986, 59.

Maupassant, Guy de. "A Piece of String." *Miss Harriet*. V. Havard, 1884.

Maxwell, Neal A. "'A Brother Offended'. " *Ensign,* May 1982, 37.

McConkie, Bruce R. *Doctrines of Salvation,* 3 volumes. Salt Lake City: Bookcraft, 1954-56.

_____. *1976 Devotional Speeches of the Year*. Provo: Brigham Young University Press, 1977.

McGraw, Phillip C. Ph.D. *Life Strategies, Doing What Works, Doing What Matters*. New York: Hyperion Books, 1999, 22.

Mc Kay, David O. "The 'Whole' Man," *Improvement Era,* April 1952, 221.

McKay, Llewelyn R. *Secrets of a Happy Life*. Comp. Salt Lake City: Bookcraft, 1967.

Merrill, Bryon R. "They Wrote to Us As If We Were Present." *Ensign*, January 2000, 13.

Monson, Thomas S."School Thy Feelings, O My Brother." *Liahona*, November 2009, 62, 67-69.

_____. "Three Goals to Guide You." *Ensign*, November 2007, 119.

Nelson, Russell M. "The Magnificence of Man." Brigham Young University Devotional, March 29, 1987.

_____. 'You Are a Child of God." *New Era*, July 2008, 2.

Newquist, Gerald L. *Gospel Truth, vol.2*. Salt Lake City: Deseret Book Company, 1974.

Our Heritage: A Brief History of The Church of Jesus Christ of Latter-day Saints. Salt Lake City: The Church of Jesus Christ of Latter–day Saints, 1966.

Packer, Boyd K. "Patriarchal Blessing of Boyd K. Packer." January 15, 1944.

_____. "Ye Are the Temple of God." *Ensign*, November 2000.

Peale, Norman Vincent. *The Power of Positive Thinking*. New York City: Prentice- Hall, 1952.

Peterson, H. Burke. "Clean Thoughts, Pure Lives." Brigham Young University Devotional, October 25, 1983.

Pearson, Carol Lynn. "The Cast." *The Growing Season*. Salt Lake City: Bookcraft, 1976.

Philadelphia Inquirer. "Among the Amish, a grace that endures." 2006.

Richards, Legrand. *A Marvelous Work and a Wonder*. Salt Lake City: Deseret Book, 1976.

Samuelson, Cecil O. "What Does It Mean to Be Perfect?" *New Era*, January 2006, 10-13.

Santayana, George. *The Life of Reason.* Volume I, 1905.

Scott, Richard G. "Peace of Conscience and Peace of Mind." *Ensign,* November 2004, 16.

_____. "The Path to Peace and Joy." *Ensign,* November 2000, 27.

Shaara, Jeff. *The Glorious Cause.* New York City: Ballantine Books, 2002.

Shakespeare, William. Act III, scene ii, *Merchant of Venice.* Act III, scene iii, *Othello.*

Smith, Eldred G. "Opposition in Order to Strengthen Us." *Ensign,* January 1974, 62.

Sandburg, Carl. "Phizzog." *Good Morning America.* 1928.

Steinbeck, John. *The Pearl.* New York City: The Viking Press, 1947.

Struthers, William M. *Wired for Intimacy, How Pornography Hijacks the Male Brain.* Downers Grove, IL: InterVarsity Press, 2009.

Tanner, Susan W. "The Sanctity of the Body." *Liahona,* November, 2005, 14.

Taylor, Gary D. *Life is Easy, I Just Decide It's Hard,* Cedar Fort: Cedar Fort Publishing, 2007.

Teachings of Presidents of the Church: Gordon B. Hinckley. Salt Lake City: The Church of Jesus Christ of Latter-day Saints, 2016.

Teachings of the Presidents of the Church: Harold B. Lee. Salt Lake City: The Church of Jesus Christ of Latter-day Saints, 2000.

Tocqueville, Alexis de. *Democracy in America.* London: Saunders and Otley, 1835.

Top, Brent L. "'Thou Shall Not Covet.'" *Ensign,* December 1994, 22.

True to the Faith. Salt Lake City: The Church of Jesus Christ of Latter-day Saints, 2004.

Uchtdorf, Dieter F. "Happiness, Your Heritage." *General Relief Society Broadcast*, October 2008.

_____. "The Reflection in the Water." CES Devotional, 2009.

Viorst, Judith. *Alexander and the Terrible, Horrible, No Good, Very Bad Day*. New York City: Atheneum Books, 1972.

Walters, Lola B. "The Grapefruit Syndrome." *Liahona*, September 1999, 24.

Watson, Elden J, comp. *Manuscript History of Brigham Young*, 1846-1847, Salt Lake City, 1971.

Widtsoe, John A. "A Rational Theology As Taught By The Church Of Jesus Christ Of Latter Day Saints" Kessinger Publishing, 2004.

Williams, Clyde J. *The Teachings of Harold B. Lee*, ed. Salt Lake City: Bookcraft, 1996.

Wirthlin, Joseph B. "Concern for the One." *Ensign*, May 2008, 19.

_____. "Press On." *Liahona,* November 2004, 101.

Whitman, Samuel T. "Forgotten Wedges." Quoted by Spencer W. Kimball, in Conference Report, April 1966.

www.brainyquote.com/ Jay S. Walker

www.cnn.com/2006/amish.shootings.

www.800padutch.com/amishvictims.shtml. "Amish Shooting Victims."

www. poemhunter.com

www.sedon.com/ grudges.

CPSIA information can be obtained
at www.ICGtesting.com
Printed in the USA
LVHW041745100220
646429LV00005B/415